# NAME & TAME Your Anxiety

## A Kid's Guide

Summer Batte

Illustrated by Amberin Huq

free spirit

PUBLISHING®

**Library of Congress Cataloging-in-Publication Data**
Names: Batte, Summer, author. | Huq, Amberin, illustrator.
Title: Name and tame your anxiety : a kid's guide / Summer Batte ; illustrated by Amberin Huq.
Description: Minneapolis : Free Spirit Publishing Inc., 2021. | Includes bibliographical references and index. | Audience: Ages 9–13
Identifiers: LCCN 2020041309 (print) | LCCN 2020041310 (ebook) | ISBN 9781631986208 (paperback) | ISBN 9781631986215 (pdf) | ISBN 9781631986222 (epub)
Subjects: LCSH: Anxiety—Juvenile literature. | Anxiety in children—Juvenile literature. | Anxiety disorders—Juvenile literature.
Classification: LCC BF575.A6 B38 2021 (print) | LCC BF575.A6 (ebook) | DDC 155.4/1246—dc23
LC record available at https://lccn.loc.gov/2020041309
LC ebook record available at https://lccn.loc.gov/2020041310]

Edited by Cassie Sitzman
Cover and interior design by Emily Dyer
Illustrated by Amberin Huq

Printed in the United States of America

**Free Spirit Publishing**
An imprint of Teacher Created Materials
6325 Sandburg Road, Suite 100
Minneapolis, MN 55427-3674
(612) 338-2068
help4kids@freespirit.com
freespirit.com

FSC
www.fsc.org
MIX
Paper from
responsible sources
FSC® C005010

**Free Spirit offers competitive pricing.**
Contact edsales@freespirit.com for pricing information on multiple quantity purchases.

# Dedication

For my daughter, who inspired me; my husband, who calmly supports everything I get myself into; my family, who are the best cheerleaders; and all the friends who asked for years when I was going to write a book. You can stop now.

# Acknowledgments

For 13 years, doctors, psychologists, therapists, teachers, and friends have made time for conversations with me as I figured out how to parent, and then educate, a child with anxiety. Every one of those conversations helped in the creation of this book, as have the dozens of books on anxiety that sit on my shelves. My thanks to Cassandra Sitzman and Free Spirit Publishing for taking on this project and guiding me through the process; to psychologist Dr. Myles Cooley for his review of the book; to family, friends, and colleagues who listened to my half-baked ideas, talked to me about their own children's struggles, read drafts of this book, or offered their advice and perspectives; and to Stanford University, my alma mater and my employer, where I learned the basics of psychology, gained the confidence to take on any subject, and developed the skills to turn what I've learned into something that can help others.

# Contents

# PART 2 Taming Anxiety

# Part 3 Talking About Anxiety

# A Note to Kids

Have you ever felt worried about something that hasn't happened yet—like a big test or your first meeting at a new club? That's anxiety! Have you ever felt uneasy or nervous about a story you've heard on the news? That's anxiety too! Maybe the feeling goes away after a little while, or maybe you have those feelings almost all the time. Everyone—kids and grown-ups—feels anxiety sometimes. But adults don't always explain anxiety or how to manage it in a way that makes sense to kids. It's important for kids to understand the science behind anxiety and know why learning to manage it can help them.

In this book, you'll learn more about anxiety and how it works in your brain and body, what you can do to feel less anxiety right now and in the future, and why some kids get help for anxiety (and what happens if you do). You'll also learn about self-advocacy, or speaking up for what you need, and how to understand and respond to some of the common things adults say about anxiety.

I recommend reading this book from beginning to end. That way you'll understand the basics of anxiety and how it works in your brain and body, and the rest of the book will make more sense. But you can also skip around to find the parts that are most helpful or interesting to you. However you choose to read this book, there are a few things to know:

- This book sometimes uses the word *parent* to mean a *trusted adult*. That could be your mom, dad, grandparent, aunt or uncle, favorite teacher, school counselor, religious or spiritual leader, stepparent, foster parent, or whoever your most trusted adults are.

- In this book, *anxiety* is most often used as a noun (rather than the adjective *anxious*). It can be helpful to think of anxiety as a *thing* we deal with rather than a part of us we can't control.

- This book uses the names of real brain parts and chemicals so you can start to understand what happens in your brain when you feel anxiety. There are more parts of the brain and chemicals involved in anxiety than we can cover in this book. This is a beginning to help you learn about the basics.

- This book explains what it means to have an anxiety disorder, what happens in therapy, and how medications for anxiety work. This doesn't mean you have to have an anxiety disorder to read the book. The strategies and information are helpful for all people who have anxiety.

- This book includes examples of things kids your age might be worried about. You may recognize some of them, and others might not worry you at all. Some may be things you were not worried about before, but now start to worry you. If these new ideas worry you, know that it's also okay to talk back to anxiety and decide to pay attention to other things instead. This book will show you how.

- As you work on managing anxiety, you'll get better at telling your brain that it's okay to calm down or think about something else. The more you practice the skills and strategies in this book, the easier they will get.

- Kids who feel a lot of anxiety are very brave—after all, you might be facing your fears every single day!

- You are ready to learn about anxiety and understand the things grown-ups are saying about it.

I hope this book helps you understand what is happening in your own body and brain when you feel anxiety. And I hope it gives you a starting point for talking with the adults who can help you get what you need to start managing anxiety.

I'd love to know what you thought was helpful in this book. Write to me to tell me what you liked or let me know about other anxiety-taming strategies you like to use.

## Summer Batte

You can email me at help4kids@freespirit.com.

Or you can send me a letter in care of:
Free Spirit Publishing
6325 Sandburg Road, Suite 100
Minneapolis, NN 55427-3674

# PART 1

## Understanding Anxiety

# What Is Anxiety?

**Anxiety** is your body's natural response to stress. It is a feeling of worry. You may feel a little bit of anxiety or a lot of it. It can alert you to danger and can help you prepare and pay attention. Like happiness, sadness, and other feelings, anxiety is part of being human. Everyone feels it sometimes. Those feelings start in our brains. But our brains and our bodies are connected. Sometimes we can determine what's happening in our brains by how our bodies react. Have you ever smiled and taken a big breath when you saw someone you love? Have you ever had a stomachache before the first day of school? Maybe you've cried when you lost something important to you or felt your heart beat fast during the scary part of a movie.

**Anxiety:**

A feeling of worry about something that could happen, something you imagine might happen, or something that happened in the past.

Those things happen in your body, but they are all reactions to feelings in your brain—happiness, sadness, and fear. When you feel anxiety, your brain can show you that feeling of worry through reactions in your body.

## How Anxiety Feels

Anxiety feels different to each person, but for most people, it causes a reaction in their body that can feel pretty uncomfortable. When we talk about body reactions that we might wish to have less often, we call them **symptoms**.

**Symptom:**

A sign or signal about what's going on in a person's brain or body.

A runny nose can be a symptom of a cold. You can't really see the cold, but you can tell your friend probably has one if his nose is runny. And your friend would probably like to have the cold and the runny-nose symptom go away. A sore throat is another common symptom of a cold. You can't really see your friend's sore throat, but he can feel it, and that's how he might know he is sick.

Symptoms of anxiety are similar—they are the ways we can tell that a brain is probably worried. Most people would like to feel anxiety less often, so we call the body reactions to anxiety "symptoms of anxiety."

Here's what some kids say anxiety feels like:

" My stomach hurts. "

" I don't want to go to school because I feel like everyone else is an alien. They are smiling while I feel worried about everything. "

" It's hard to pay attention to a conversation. I miss a lot of what people say, and then I feel confused and even more anxious. "

" My brain keeps saying the same things over and over. I can't make it stop and it makes it hard to fall asleep. "

" It feels like at any moment something bad might happen. I'm waiting for it to happen, but it doesn't. "

We can't see anxiety because it's a feeling, not a physical thing. You *can* see a cold, technically, because it's a virus. But you'd need a great microscope, so most of us rely on knowing the symptoms. Most anxiety symptoms cannot be seen by others. A racing heart or headache is probably not visible to friends. But the person experiencing these symptoms can feel them.

## Anxiety Symptoms

There are lots of possible symptoms of anxiety. Here are some of them:

- upset stomach
- headache
- trouble sleeping
- biting nails
- trouble focusing or paying attention
- not wanting to go to school
- crying more than usual
- getting angry at people you care about (not just your brother!)
- sweaty hands
- racing heart
- fear of leaving your parent
- fast breathing or a feeling like you can't get enough air
- confusion
- trouble sitting still
- keep thinking about bad things that could happen

- checking things over and over to make sure they are right
- trouble speaking when a teacher calls on you
- just don't feel right

You may have felt one of these symptoms of anxiety or many of them, or you may have had different symptoms. You might wonder how we know that these are signs of anxiety. Sometimes, it can be hard to know. But if you pay attention to the times you feel these symptoms, you can start to notice patterns. For example, if you get a stomachache before one swim lesson, it's probably just a stomachache. (Stomachs can be weird like that.) But if you get a stomachache before *every* swim lesson—it's happening over and over—then it's probably anxiety.

It can help to talk about your symptoms with a trusted adult (such as a parent or stepparent, a teacher or school counselor, or a coach). This person can help you decide whether a feeling is a symptom of anxiety or something else. In chapter 4, you'll learn ways to help yourself with those feelings and symptoms too.

## Can Other People Tell That You Are Feeling Anxiety?

Some symptoms of anxiety—such as biting your nails—might be visible. Other symptoms—such as a pounding heart—are only felt by the person experiencing them. Often, other people can't tell that you are feeling anxiety. And you probably can't tell that they are feeling anxiety either. If it's the first day of the new school year and you feel very worried about being with a new teacher and new classmates, you might look around to see if other kids are feeling the same way. You might decide that nobody else is feeling anxiety or having worries because they are not showing symptoms that you can see. But here's a secret: *lots of them are worried*! (It's common to feel anxiety in new situations or when you try new things.) You just might not be able to see the symptoms of anxiety that the other kids are experiencing. They may also be using some handy tricks to calm themselves down and to remind themselves that they are safe. You can learn those things too. We call them **strategies**, and you can read more about them on pages 60-66.

## Strategy:

Something you can do to help your brain know that everything is okay and it can calm down now.

# Words That Mean Anxiety

Everyone feels anxiety. But we don't often hear it called *anxiety*. If you listen, you might hear people say. . .

> . . . I'm **nervous** about a test.

> . . . I feel **scared** to go somewhere new.

> . . . I'm **worried** about giving a speech.

> . . . I feel **overwhelmed** or **stressed** about how much work I have to do.

> . . . I **can't** do this.

You may have felt these things too. Maybe you feel . . .

> . . . **nervous** about playing well in the big game.

> . . . **scared** about something happening to your family.

> . . . **worried** that your classmates are still thinking about a mistake you made.

> . . . **overwhelmed** or **stressed** about remembering your lines in the school play.

> . . . like you **just can't** go to school again.

These are all examples of anxiety. And these words are ways of saying "I'm feeling anxiety." It happens to everybody. And with good reason. Anxiety is your brain's way of telling you to be careful. But sometimes our brains overreact, misunderstand, or can't calm down, making us feel anxiety longer, more intensely, or more often than we need to.

# When Anxiety Starts to Get in the Way

Everyone has feelings of anxiety sometimes, but some people have feelings of anxiety much more often than others do, and their feelings—or symptoms—are more **intense**. If anxiety starts to make it difficult for you to do the things you want to do (such as hang out at your friend's house) or need to do (such as go to school), your parents may take you to the doctor. It could be the doctor you are used to seeing for your check-ups, or it could be someone new. If anxiety is getting in the way at school, a teacher may suggest that you talk with a school counselor or school psychologist.

**Intense:**
A word commonly used when talking about symptoms. It means the strength of the symptom. We can use intensity to describe other things too. The sound of a mother singing to her baby is quiet, not a very intense sound. But the sound of a lawnmower near you is very intense!

The doctor will ask questions about your symptoms and their intensity. She may ask how you feel about school, what you like to do with friends, and what you and your family like to do at home. You can be totally honest during this conversation. Sometimes kids think they should answer that they like school (or raising their hand in class or going to birthday parties) because grown-ups want them to like these things. But adults need to hear how you really feel so they can help with your anxiety. Grown-ups are generally pretty sturdy—they can handle it!

> "The doctor asked how I feel when I get to school. I don't know what the feeling is. I just don't like it."

It can be difficult to explain the feelings in your brain. Instead, try to describe what happens in your body. Maybe your muscles feel tight or it becomes hard to hear what people are saying to you. Maybe you start to feel hot or sick, or you get tired and want to cover your head.

The doctor may also do a few things you are used to, like looking in your ears and listening to your heart. She may have you take a blood test (which may sound scary but is very quick and very safe). She is doing these tests to rule out any physical problems that may be causing your symptoms.

After talking to you and reviewing the tests, your doctor may give you a **diagnosis**. You may be diagnosed with an anxiety **disorder**. You can ask the doctor to explain what your anxiety disorder means and whether other kids have it. (They do. In fact, 4.4 million kids in the United States have been diagnosed with an anxiety disorder. That's a lot of kids!) The doctor may recommend you see a counselor, therapist, or another doctor. She will also talk with you and your parents about **treatment**.

## Diagnosis:

An official name for the cause of your symptoms, given by an expert.

## Disorder:

A word to mean that something is not working the way we would hope. Sort of the opposite of order. But not like ordering a burrito. You can't dis-order a burrito. Besides, why would you want to?

## Treatment:

Working with a doctor, counselor, or therapist on learning to manage anxiety or another challenge.

Whether or not you have an anxiety disorder, you might wonder if you'll always struggle with anxiety. Each person is different, but when anxiety starts to get in the way, it doesn't usually just go away on its own. However, you can learn to manage your anxiety more often. Many people who learn to manage their anxiety feel pretty great most of the time.

## What Anxiety Is and Is Not

- Anxiety is not a sign that you are broken.

- Anxiety is something every person feels from time to time. Some people have an anxiety disorder.

- Anxiety is not something we want to go away completely. A little bit of anxiety can help you do your best on a test or before a performance and can keep you safe.

- Anxiety is exhausting to feel too much of. Learning how to manage it can make you feel a lot better.

- Anxiety is not a sign that you are not smart. People of all intelligence levels have anxiety.

- Anxiety is not contagious like a cold. You can't catch it by being around another person with anxiety.

- Anxiety is something that can be passed down through families. If you have anxiety, there's a good chance someone else in your family also does.

- Anxiety is not your fault. Getting help with anxiety is a positive and brave thing to do.

# 2  What Causes Anxiety?

For millions of years, the brains of animals have been sensing danger and reacting to it. You've probably seen a bird get worried. It pokes around on the ground when suddenly, it looks up, wide-eyed, and flies off. That bird probably heard or saw something that its brain thought was dangerous—like an approaching predator—and flew away to escape. Over millions of years, the brains of animals have developed to be very, very good at this. Humans have become great at it too. In fact, we have a section of the brain dedicated to alerting us to danger. It's small and in the middle of our brains. It's called the amygdala (uh-MIG-duh-lah).

Many, *many* years ago, there were no video games, no schools, no houses with locks on the doors, no doctors or prescriptions, no firefighters, and no grocery stores with food in them. Humans survived by hunting and gathering, and they needed to be very aware of the dangers in their world. Those dangers were serious—back then, humans had fewer ways to stay healthy and safe. An infection or a broken bone could be life-threatening. With no medicine and much less understanding of how to keep the body healthy, early humans died of things we can treat easily today.

Because the world was a much more dangerous place for early humans, it was a very good thing that the amygdala became an expert at recognizing potential danger and reacting quickly.

In fact, the human amygdala got really, *really* good at this. It is the biggest worrier ever. Its mission in life is to keep you safe. But it still thinks you are living in prehistoric times. It can't tell the difference between something that is actually happening and is truly dangerous and something that you are just thinking about—imagining. It's why everyone feels anxiety at times.

The amygdala is not the smartest part of your brain.

**Fact!** You actually have two amygdalae (uh-MIG-duh-lee, plural for amygdala), one for each side of your brain. They are almond-shaped and close to each other. Since they work as one, we'll just talk about them like they are one amygdala.

Your amygdala relies on other parts of your brain to send it messages to calm down. It can help to think of the parts of your brain like a team. Each part has an important job to do, and they need to communicate with each other to be a great team and keep things running smoothly. Sometimes all those parts of the brain have a hard time communicating. When that happens, not every section has all the information it needs, and they can't all work together. (What if you told a relay team to run a race, but didn't communicate what leg of the race each team member should run? When the race starts, you might have two teammates waiting at the third leg and no one to catch the baton from the first runner.)

# When People Feel Anxiety

All people get worried. Sometimes that feeling of anxiety goes away pretty quickly. For example, you might hear something on the news that sounds scary and feel very anxious about it. After talking to an adult about how the scary thing happened far away from where you live, you might feel your body and brain calm down, allowing you to get back to focusing on things you like to do. Or you might worry all morning about going to the dentist—but after the appointment is over, you feel relieved and happier. Most people feel anxiety in some situations for a short period of time. It's annoying and uncomfortable, but it doesn't cause a big problem.

But sometimes people continue to feel a lot of anxiety after hearing about something worrisome or start to worry weeks before that dentist appointment. In these situations, anxiety is annoying and uncomfortable, *and* it is probably starting to interfere with the rest of the person's life. Anxiety is starting to cause a problem. A person who experiences this might have an anxiety disorder.

Sometimes people develop an anxiety disorder after a particular frightening event. They might be bitten by a dog and develop a fear (sometimes called a phobia) of dogs. Or a kid might be separated from a parent who was in the hospital, and afterward may become worried about being away from that parent.

In other cases, there is no particular scary or worrisome event that happened. Some kids with anxiety disorders say they've always felt worried. It's just the way their brains work. In those cases, adults might say the kid inherited anxiety or that it's "hereditary."

# Heredity

Heredity is the passing of physical or mental traits from one generation to the next. We pass these traits via our genes, or DNA. Eye color is based on heredity; so is curly or straight hair. Heredity is different from something being contagious. You can't give blue eyes to a friend. What examples of heredity can you think of in your family?

Brain skills—like recognizing danger—have been handed down from every parent to every child for many generations. That's why everyone can feel worried or anxious. But some people have an amygdala that is *very excellent* at this job, or other parts of their brain have a hard time telling the amygdala to calm down. And that can be shared in families as well. That means if you feel a lot of anxiety, there is a good chance someone else in your family has had similar experiences.

Perhaps your mother or father has an anxiety disorder. Or maybe a grandparent wasn't ever diagnosed but had a lot of symptoms of anxiety. They may have been called "nervous" or "sensitive" or "very shy." There's a chance those people had an anxiety disorder. Just like you are always learning new things at school, scientists are always learning more about the brain. Still, even today, many people who have an anxiety disorder are not diagnosed.

## Big Worries

In our modern world, we may not have the same concerns that early humans had, but kids and adults today still have real worries, and some of them are about BIG topics. You may worry about issues your family is dealing with or things that are happening in your neighborhood or school. You might also have a lot of access to information about the larger world—online or through TV—that causes you to worry about events happening far away or about things that could affect people in the future. You might see adults showing signs that they are also worried about these things. Worrying about big things doesn't necessarily mean you have an anxiety disorder. But for people who do struggle with anxiety, big worries can be especially hard to handle.

Any feelings you have are okay, and you are not the only kid who has them. These big problems are usually complicated, and there might not be much you can do to solve them right now. Even if you can't fix the problem, you can find ways to feel better. It's a good idea to talk to a trusted adult about these worries. Adults can help explain what's going on, and they might have more information that will help you feel safe and less worried. They might also be able to help you come up with an idea for something you can do to help out in your community. You can also use some of strategies in chapter 4 for managing anxiety when you're feeling worried about big things.

# When Anxiety Is Good

There's a very good reason we can all feel anxiety—it's really helpful sometimes! If you are about to step into the street but see a car coming toward you, you might feel your heart speed up and a wave of heat go through your body as you quickly step back onto the sidewalk. That was your amygdala doing its job and keeping you safe. If you've ever touched a hot stove, you probably try never to do it again (it hurts!). When you see a hot stove, your amygdala remembers hot stoves hurt, and can remind you with a little bit of anxiety.

Anxiety is also useful when you need to prepare for something—like the school play or a math test. A little anxiety can make you feel worried about not doing well, and that can motivate you to rehearse your lines or practice math problems.

# When Anxiety Is a Problem

When does good or helpful anxiety start to become a problem? Consider this example: A little bit of anxiety about your plant dying might help you remember to water it before you leave to visit your grandparents for a week. Too much worry about your plant, and you might overwater it, resulting in a big mess and an unhappy plant.

When your brain overreacts to anxiety, can't stop worrying, or worries out of proportion to the danger (like watering your houseplant with a fire hose), then anxiety can become a problem. It can make it very difficult for you to relax, have fun, or learn. You deserve to be able to hear and think about what your teacher is saying, feel calm during a conversation with friends, or play your favorite game and just have fun. When anxiety stops you from doing these things, it's time to learn ways to get it under control.

# What's Happening in Your Brain

Your brain is complicated. So complicated that scientists don't yet understand all of it. But they do know this: the brain has lots of sections, each involved in different tasks. The sections communicate with each other and with the rest of your body. The way the brain communicates with your body and with itself is similar to sending letters through the mail. (This probably sounds super old-school, but it's a good metaphor.) The letters are messages that help each part of the brain understand what's going on and when to do their special jobs.

These letters (or brain messages) help the sections of your brain work like a team. Three important players are the amygdala, the hypothalamus, and the prefrontal cortex. You've already met the amygdala, but let's learn more about it and how it works with the rest of the team.

## THE AMYGDALA

A small section in the middle of the brain. But don't let its tiny size fool you. It is responsible for feeling big emotions, including fear and sadness, and for alerting you to danger.

**Goal:** To make sure you survive. It thinks you are living in prehistoric times with lions chasing you and threats everywhere. It hasn't caught up to the fact that you're in the 21st century.

**Strengths:** Keeps you safe; can help motivate you to prepare for big events.

**Weaknesses:** Always wants to be the center of attention; can overreact; can't tell the difference between what's real, what's imaginary, and what's possible but not actually happening.

**MOTTO** "LOOK AT ME! LOOK AT ME!"

# THE PREFRONTAL CORTEX

This section leads the way. Literally—it's the front of your brain. It solves problems and makes decisions. When you think about thinking (also called metacognition), you are using your prefrontal cortex.

**Goal:** To be in charge, helping you learn along the way.

**Strengths:** Very smart. This section solves problems and makes decisions about how to respond to anything that happens to you or that you think about.

**Weaknesses:** Sometimes overthinks decisions; might need some training to talk back to the amygdala.

**MOTTO** "I CAN HANDLE THIS."

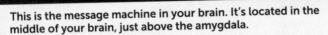

## THE HYPOTHALAMUS

This is the message machine in your brain. It's located in the middle of your brain, just above the amygdala.

**Goal:** To receive messages from other sections of the brain and send orders to the body about how to respond—with a faster heartbeat, sweat, goose bumps, staying very still and quiet, or whatever the situation calls for.

**Strengths:** Reacts quickly; great at letting the team know what's going on.

**Weaknesses:** Can't really make decisions on its own; only does what the messages say.

**MOTTO** "I JUST DO WHAT THEY TELL ME."

# How the Parts of the Brain Work Together

Now that you've met the different parts of your brain, let's talk about how they work together to send and receive messages about anxiety. Pretend you're out walking at the park, when suddenly you come upon a roaring lion. Your amygdala would believe you are in danger and would send out brain messages that **THERE'S A LION AND WE SHOULD FREAK OUT NOW.**

Your hypothalamus receives that message and sends out chemical messages to your body to prepare for danger—making you breathe quickly, having your heart pump fast so you can run or fight, and pausing systems you won't be needing right now, like digestion. (Because who has time to eat when there's a lion right there?)

## Fight, Flight, or Freeze

Your amygdala just wants to keep you safe; your hypothalamus just wants to be ready. And since they're not very smart, they only know three ways to do that. When your amygdala thinks you might be in danger, there are three types of reactions you can have: fight, flight, or freeze. This is called your brain's fight-or-flight response. Many of the symptoms of anxiety are the result of your brain getting your body ready to do these things.

**Fight:** Your brain has decided you should try to fight back against the danger. (Symptoms: pounding heart; tingling or jittery muscles)

**Flight:** Your brain has decided you should run away from the danger. (Symptoms: fast breathing; feeling of wanting to escape)

**Freeze:** Your brain has decided you should stay very still and quiet, sort of like how an animal might hide in hopes that a predator will lose interest and go away. (Symptoms: feel stuck; can't talk)

You might start running automatically when you see the lion. That's because your amygdala has taken control. But your prefrontal cortex also gets the message about the lion. And the prefrontal cortex can make smarter decisions. The prefrontal cortex sends messages to ask the hypothalamus to please quiet things down a bit so you can think. You're still worried, but your breathing might slow a little and you might be able to see things besides the lion again—like the playground nearby. Then the prefrontal cortex can check things out. Is this a real danger or something that is possible but not actually happening? As you look more closely at the lion, you realize it's a statue. It's not real.

Your prefrontal cortex does something *really important* then—it sends messages back to the other sections of the brain. These messages say, "Thank you. There's no real danger here. You can calm down now." Your hypothalamus sends messages to your body to rest. You stop sweating; your heart beats more slowly. Your amygdala calms down, and you feel relaxed and able to think about things besides lions.

At least, that's how it's supposed to work.

You probably know some kids at school who could see an actual lion, get freaked out, and then go have lunch like nothing ever happened. (What is up with that?) And you know that some brains don't react like that. Some brains are fantastic—truly spectacular!—at getting worried, or afraid, or stuck. Those brains seem to have an easier time becoming worried and have a harder time calming down and feeling relaxed again. Why is that?

Well, did you notice how many messages had to be sent back and forth in the lion situation? A lot.

What would happen if there weren't enough messages getting delivered between sections of your brain?

What if your amygdala freaked out over smaller, non-lion things (because it can) like homework? Or things that haven't even happened yet, like spending the night away from your parents or finding a spider in your room? Or things that are unlikely to happen at all, like the possibility of getting into a car accident?

What if your amygdala learned so well from its lion experience that now it panics every time you see a statue? Or any time you remember the lion episode?

What if your prefrontal cortex tries to send messages back to say that everything's okay—but the messages don't get through?

## REAL QUESTIONS FROM REAL KIDS

**"Why can some messages get through but not others?"**

The brain uses many types of messages. The ones that turn ON your fight-or-flight response aren't the same as the messages that turn OFF anxiety or worry. That's why you might have an easy time becoming anxious but a hard time stopping those feelings.

If your amygdala can't calm down or alerts you to "danger" too often, it would be active or "on" a lot of the time. You'd feel afraid, upset, or worried much more than you needed to. Your hypothalamus would keep your heart rate elevated more often. You'd feel all jittery and ready to run. This can make it hard to focus on what your teacher is saying or what your friends are doing. You might feel confused about why the people around you aren't panicked. You would feel anxiety more often than you need to.

And all because of some lost messages and poor communication in your brain.

How does this happen? One or more of the following could be occurring:

- The parts of the brain are having trouble delivering their messages.

- The brain isn't making enough of the right messages.

- The brain is too good at cleaning out the messages, kind of like throwing the mail away before you've had a chance to read it.

How can you change what's happening? You have to make sure the amygdala gets the calm-down messages. There are several ways to do that. We'll talk about them in chapter 4 (page 42).

FROM: PREFRONTAL CORTEX

To: AMYGDALA

ADDRESS UNKNOWN

# Types of Anxiety

There are some common symptoms (or feelings) of anxiety that many people have. There are also some common things lots of people worry about (like giving a presentation in class). But generally, the situations that switch on anxiety and the symptoms people experience are not the same for everyone.

Imagine anxiety is allergies. There are many types of allergies (to foods, animals, and more), just like there are many types of anxiety. One person may be allergic to cats and start sneezing around them. Another person may be fine around cats but be allergic to nuts, which give them itchy hives. Both people have symptoms of an allergy, but what switches on their allergy and what symptoms they have are very different. How they treat their symptoms can be very different too. Someone who's allergic to cats may take an allergy pill if they are going to visit a relative who has a pet cat, while someone who is allergic to nuts has to avoid any foods that contain nuts.

# Common Types of Anxiety

To help in understanding and treating anxiety, experts have made categories of anxiety (kind of like types of allergies). Several are common among kids who have anxiety. Maybe you know which category fits you the best, or maybe you fit into a few categories.

As you read about these different types of anxiety, you might recognize things you've felt or experienced. That doesn't always mean you have an anxiety disorder. Knowing more about the common types of anxiety can help you understand how you are feeling. It can also help you talk with adults about the kinds of anxiety you experience most often.

## Generalized Anxiety

Kids with generalized anxiety disorder (GAD) are worried about many things. An adult might say the kid worries "**excessively**." While most people may worry a little bit about the possibility of crashing their bike, a person with GAD might worry about it so much that they won't ride their bike. Usually people with GAD are worried about a lot of things, like family issues, whether their friends like them, school, dying, or doing well in a soccer game. They worry about these things so much that it makes it difficult for them to do activities or to relax and have fun. To lessen their feelings of anxiety, kids with GAD might try to do everything perfectly or frequently ask adults for reassurance that everything is okay.

## Excessive:

In excess, or more than needed. A person who puts 10 scoops of mashed potatoes on her plate has an excessive amount of potatoes, or more than most people would consider a reasonable amount for one person to eat. Excessive worry is more worry than most people would consider reasonable for the situation.

## Separation Anxiety

Many kids feel some anxiety on the first day of school or for a few minutes when they go to a sleepover. Kids with separation anxiety have more intense or frequent anxiety about being away from their parents (or other trusted people). These kids may grab onto their parent's arm every day at school. They might be afraid that something bad will happen while they are apart, or a past event might make a kid worried that their parent won't be there when they get home. It may feel difficult or impossible for kids with separation anxiety to go on a field trip or visit grandparents without their mom or dad.

## Social Anxiety

Making friends and answering a question in front of the whole class can make many people a little nervous. But kids with social anxiety disorder have a big fear of speaking up in class, performing, or talking to other people. They can feel like everyone is watching them. They may worry that other kids think or say negative things about them. This can make it much harder for kids with social anxiety to be in school, join a new team, make friends, or talk to the doctor about a sore throat.

## Selective Mutism

Some kids find they cannot speak in certain situations. For example, kids with selective mutism might be big chatterboxes at home (or other places where they are comfortable) but unable to speak at school. They may also look away from people who are talking to them. This fear of speaking makes it difficult to make and keep friends and difficult to get help from teachers or other adults.

## Specific Phobias

A phobia is an extreme or **irrational** fear of a particular thing. This feeling of fear—even if it's irrational—is very real. Kids can have specific phobias of anything, but common ones include animals, water, storms, heights, the dark,

and medical procedures (like getting a shot at the doctor's office). Lots of people feel some anxiety about these things. But kids with a specific phobia feel more severe anxiety symptoms and may go to great lengths to avoid the thing they are afraid of.

Doesn't it feel good to know there are other people like you?

## Irrational:

Unreasonable, or not using "good sense." Say there is a short path to school that takes 5 minutes and a long path that takes 15 minutes. If a kid who is afraid of water insists on the longer path to avoid taking a bridge over water, they are making their own life more difficult in order to avoid doing something most people consider safe. Over time, that fear of water can become worse, and the kid may have to do many extra, inconvenient things to avoid water. It makes life more difficult than it needs to be, and therefore doesn't make good sense. It's irrational.

## Panic Disorder

Kids with panic disorder have short periods of time (minutes to hours) where they suddenly feel dizzy, like they can't get enough breath, and even like they might be dying. These are called panic attacks or anxiety attacks. Kids having a panic attack usually feel an intense need to run away from the place where the attack is happening, even though there is actually nothing to be afraid of in the situation. A panic attack is an example of the amygdala sending a false alarm for danger. Although there is no real danger, panic attacks still feel very scary. Kids who have them often avoid places where they've had panic attacks in the past and may start avoiding any place where they feel they can't escape (usually crowded or enclosed places).

## Obsessive-Compulsive Disorder (OCD)

Have you ever heard someone say they are "obsessed" with a video game? They usually mean they can't stop thinking about it. Usually people are exaggerating when they say they are obsessed. But kids with OCD have negative or worrying thoughts that stay in their brains, and they can't seem to stop them. They may think a thought over and over—adults might say kids "ruminate" on the thought. The thoughts might be about a parent dying or about needing to do things "just right," and they make kids feel very anxious.

Some kids with OCD have compulsive behaviors they do to try to get relief from their nagging thoughts. Compulsive means feeling that they *have to* do the behavior. A kid with OCD might worry about leaving their locker unlocked during the day. They might think that if they leave their locker open, something bad will happen. These thoughts worry them, so they may want to check their locker to stop the worrying thoughts. It might work for a little while, but then the worry comes back, so they check the locker again. They may do this so often that they are late for class and get in trouble at school. OCD can make it very difficult to enjoy fun times, or to do basic things that kids need to do.

Did you notice that all these types of anxiety can make it harder to do everyday things or to relax and have fun?

Did you notice that all these types of anxiety have to do with worry about something that *could* happen or that you might *imagine* happening? None of them are about actual dangers right now, like a real lion standing right in front of you. Knowing what kinds of anxiety you experience most often can help you prepare for times when anxiety might try to take control and make a plan for what you can do when anxiety strikes.

# PART 2

## Taming Anxiety

Our brains have a natural reaction to things that make us anxious. We avoid them! This makes sense sometimes. Touching a hot stove and getting burned creates an association in your brain—you link the pain of a burn with the thing that you touched. When you next see a stove, you remember the pain and you make sure that the stove isn't hot before you touch it. That's a big part of how our brains learn, and it's very effective. But as you learned in chapter 2, the amygdala can't tell the difference between true danger right now and something you imagine might happen. While it is certainly possible the stove could be hot, you know now to be careful when you're near it. You probably don't need to worry about being burned again even though you can imagine it happening.

Your brain can associate all kinds of things. If you are woken up one night by a loud and scary thunderstorm, your brain might associate sleeping in your room with bad storms. Your smart prefrontal cortex knows this doesn't make sense. The weather doesn't change because of where you sleep. It wasn't your bedroom's fault, and it probably won't storm again tonight. But your amygdala can only understand simple things, and to it:

$$bedroom = thunderstorm$$

Unless you can help the parts of your brain communicate, you may start to feel worried about sleeping in your room, even though it can't cause a thunderstorm. This is an example of anxiety being in charge when it shouldn't be.

## How a Little Healthy Fear Can Turn into a Big Anxiety

After learning that a hot stove could burn you, a **proportional** amount of worry would help you decide to check for heat before touching the stove. Your amygdala would send worry messages when you got near the stove. Then your prefrontal cortex would do some smart reasoning and let the other parts of your brain know that everything is okay: the stove is only dangerous if it is hot. Your amygdala would receive those messages and calm down. All of this would happen within seconds.

## Proportional:

A reaction size that "matches" the size of what is happening. If you encounter something that is low on the danger scale, a proportional amount of worry is also low. A disproportional amount of worry is a lot of worry about something that is not very dangerous or not very likely to happen.

A disproportional amount of worry would be avoiding the whole kitchen because the stove might be hot. That is an imagined fear—that even going into the same room as the stove might somehow result in a burn. Your prefrontal cortex can reason that going into the kitchen is not dangerous, and that the stove is only dangerous to touch if it is hot. But if your prefrontal cortex can't communicate that to your amygdala, your amygdala keeps sending out messages to get away from the kitchen. Your hypothalamus gets these worry messages and sends out commands to your body to get ready for danger. Your body starts having symptoms of anxiety.

If you don't train your brain to manage anxiety, your amygdala thinks it is correct to worry so much about getting burned. The imagined fear will get stronger and stronger. You may start to worry about the stove a lot—even when you are nowhere near the kitchen.

A good way to know if anxiety is taking control is to notice if you're thinking a lot of "what if" thoughts: "What if the stove is hot?" "What if I somehow get burned even if it's not hot?"

# Times Anxiety Likes to Take Control

When do you feel anxiety? Is it often at a certain time of day? Or is it when you are at a certain place? Knowing when anxiety is likely to happen can be helpful for a few reasons:

- Knowing when to expect anxiety gives you a good clue when you are trying to determine whether or not you're in real danger.
- It can help you explain what you feel to your trusted adults.
- It can help you and your trusted adults figure out how to help you feel less anxiety.

Here are some common times you may feel anxiety:

**When things change.** This could be a big change, like moving to a new town, or a small change, like leaving your house to go to school in the morning. Adults might use the word *transition*, which means whenever one thing is ending and another is beginning. Our brains have to do a lot of work to transition (like remembering how the rules are different at school than they are at home). That can make your amygdala activate and send messages that it thinks there is danger.

**When you are tired.** Being tired makes everything your smart brain (the prefrontal cortex) does harder, including math, baseball, being nice to your siblings, and keeping anxiety from taking over. This is also why bedtime is a common time to have symptoms of anxiety—you're tired *and* you're transitioning from daytime activities to going to sleep.

Have you ever tried to play a game with someone the day after she has been at a sleepover? She didn't get enough sleep, and now she's acting grumpy and getting frustrated easily. Sleep is really important to keep our brains working well.

**When you don't know the plan.** It can be alarming to not know what is going to happen. You might not know what you'll do on a vacation or what will happen at a birthday party. Adults call this having trouble with "uncertainty" or difficultly "not being in control." It all just means you worry when you don't know what to expect (and we all do this).

**When you try new things.** Going to a dance class for the first time, meeting a new neighbor, and eating new foods can all cause anxiety. They are changes, and because they're new, you don't know what to expect.

**When you are hungry.** Our brains and bodies evolved to make finding food a priority. So when your body needs energy (food), your amygdala may go on high alert. Some people might not even know they are hungry. They just become more anxious, sad, or angry—or all three. Go grab a banana!

**Good news!** Everyone feels some anxiety at these times.

**More good news!** You can learn ways to manage anxiety during these times and others so that you don't miss out on excitement and fun and so you don't feel such intense symptoms of anxiety.

# Benefits of Learning to Manage Anxiety

You might wonder what learning to "manage anxiety" really means. It means training your brain to calm your amygdala. Just like it takes time for an athlete to train her body, it will take time to train your brain. Managing your anxiety does *not* mean becoming okay with feeling or being unsafe. It means stopping anxiety from being in charge. It means learning to understand why you feel worried, and then giving you (and your smart prefrontal cortex) the power to decide what to do and how to be safe.

 Worrying helps me stay safe. I don't understand why adults want me to be less safe.

Experts know from lots of experience with and research about anxiety that if you don't learn to manage it, anxiety (and the amygdala) will try to be in control more and more of the time, and will associate more and more things with worry and fear. Adults still want you to be safe. But they want you to try the strategies for managing anxiety—little by little—so that YOU (and not your amygdala) can stay in control and become really good at keeping yourself safe. Managing your anxiety helps you make sure anxiety isn't taking charge when it doesn't need to. It also makes it easier for you to do the things in life you need and want to do. Lots of people who've learned to take control back from anxiety say that managing their anxiety has helped them enjoy life more.

# Keeping Your Brain and Body Healthy

You may hear your parents, teachers, and other adults talk about keeping your brain and body healthy. You may even hear them say that things like exercise and sleep can help you manage anxiety. Why is that? Well, just like your brain affects how your body works, how you treat your body can affect how your brain works. They are connected! Here are some of the common but odd-sounding things that can help you manage anxiety.

## Sleep

Remember how we said that bedtime is a common time to feel anxiety? That's because your brain is tired from the day. You might be thinking, "I don't feel tired," or "I feel tired, but I can't fall asleep." It's possible not to *feel* tired but still have a brain that is exhausted from all the work it did during the day.

Sleep is important. While you sleep, your brain does its homework so you'll be ready for the next day. It goes through all the things you did that day and stores important memories. It makes associations between things, like that having a friend come over is fun. It even sends out assignments to the rest of your body to help your muscles and bones be ready for tomorrow. If you don't get enough sleep, or don't get enough good-quality sleep, this homework piles up on your brain's desk. The next day, your brain gets more work to do, but it still hasn't finished up the work from the night before. If it never has enough time to finish everything, the pile gets higher and higher. Sleep scientists call this pile-up of work your "sleep debt." It's the amount of sleep you "owe" your brain so that it can finish all its work. A couple things that affect anxiety happen when you don't get enough sleep.

**You have symptoms of fatigue (or tiredness).** Symptoms can include yawning a lot, zoning out more, or acting cranky. It might be difficult to enjoy things you usually like. You might make more mistakes or become a bit clumsy.

**Your amygdala becomes more active.** Scientists who study brains have found that when people don't get enough good-quality sleep, their amygdala turns on more often and doesn't communicate as well with other brain areas. Not enough sleep means more anxiety.

So if getting enough sleep can make you less anxious, how much sleep do you need? The American Academy of Pediatrics recommends that kids get 9 to 12 hours of sleep per night. Every person is a bit different, so even if you are getting 9 hours of sleep, you may need more. If you're not sure whether you are getting enough sleep, try keeping a sleep journal. Write down what time you go to bed and wake up. You can add notes to the journal about the quality of your sleep—such as whether you had a hard time falling asleep or felt tired during the day. Looking at your journal after a week might give you some clues about whether you are getting enough sleep.

## Tips for Getting a Good Night's Sleep

How can you get more sleep? And how can you make sure that you are getting good-quality sleep? Parents and doctors can help you with this, but here are some tips that work for many people.

**Go to sleep and wake up at the same time every day** (even on weekends) so you get the amount of sleep you need each night. This helps train your brain to know when it's time to calm down and go to sleep.

**Turn off your electronic devices.** The kind of light that screens give off is called blue light. Blue light causes your brain to send messages to wake up. For at least one hour before bed, turn off screens and do something else. If you absolutely can't be off screens for the hour before bed, or if you use your phone as your alarm, try turning down the brightness of the screen in the evening and turning on the "night shift" or "night light" setting. This will change the screen to give off less blue light. Getting more sunlight in the morning and creating a short bedtime ritual like drinking some chamomile tea or warm milk might also help you fall asleep at night even if you can't turn off screens.

**Do calm (or even boring) stuff.** The screens are off, and this is a good time to do something mellow. Read a book that's kind of interesting, but not full of exciting action or scary stuff. Listen to classical music. Do some simple stretches. Maybe even practice some math problems you've already mastered.

**Write down your thoughts.** If you can't stop thinking about things when you are trying to fall asleep, you can help get the thoughts out of your head by writing them down. Keep a pencil and notepad or journal by your bed and jot down anything that is worrying you. You can also make a to-do list for the next day. In the morning, you'll be able to read your list and remember anything you need to do or that you felt was important enough to worry about. Sometimes things you were very worried about last night don't seem so serious in the morning. This may be because your brain was tired and worrying extra at night.

## Exercise

It may sound silly that exercising your body helps manage anxiety in your brain. Are adults just trying to get you to do more PE? Actually, no! Exercise really can help lower anxiety. A couple things that affect anxiety happen when you exercise.

**You produce chemical brain messages.** Exercise produces several kinds of messages: some that tell your brain it's okay to calm down, others that make you feel motivated and able to focus, and still others that simply make your brain feel happy. Calm, focused, and happier—all from exercise.

**You give your body a chance to burn off the fight-or-flight messages your amygdala sends.** If you feel tense, jittery, or like you can't stay still, it may be because your brain has sent your body messages that it's anxious and wants to run or fight to keep you safe. If you really do go for a jog or bike ride, play some basketball, swim, or move your body in some other way, you do what your brain wants—without running away from the thing that worried you. Your brain will feel satisfied and your body may feel much calmer. Experts recommend that kids get at least 60 minutes of physical activity each day. It's good to do a variety of activities to strengthen your heart (running), bones (jumping), and muscles (climbing a jungle gym or rock wall).

**Bonus!** Regular exercise keeps your brain functioning at its best and strengthens your body (especially really important parts like your heart) so that you can live a long, healthy life.

## What Kind of Exercise Works?

Just about any exercise works to help you manage anxiety. You can exercise with a team or your family, or you can do it alone. You don't need to get all sweaty to manage anxiety, but if you *do* sweat and it's a little bit hard to talk (because you need to breathe faster), then you are likely making even more positive brain messages than if you were exercising less intensely.

Here are some ways to exercise:

- walk or run
- swim
- ride a bike
- jump rope
- play catch (if you don't have a ball, you can use balled-up socks)
- put on some music and dance
- wash windows or mop the floors (you use a lot of muscle doing big chores, and the adults in your home will swoon with happiness)

# Mindfulness

You might have heard that mindfulness can help you manage anxiety. Some schools even make mindfulness a part of students' days. Maybe you're already familiar with mindfulness, or maybe you're wondering what exactly it is.

Mindfulness is the opposite of anxiety. Anxiety is always trying to make you think about the future (what might happen) or the past (what did happen and how you felt). Mindfulness is learning to focus only on the present—what is happening right now and how you feel about it.

To be mindful means to be focused on the present instead of thinking (or worrying) about something that already happened or things that might happen in the future. When someone practices mindfulness, it means that they are doing an activity that helps them focus on the present. It might be a bit difficult to understand at first, but give it a try. Mindfulness has been shown to decrease anxiety. A couple things happen when you practice mindfulness.

**You exercise your prefrontal cortex**—the part of your brain that controls attention, problem-solving, and decision-making. That part of the brain becomes stronger over time and can better help you focus your attention on things other than worries.

**You teach yourself how to have feelings and thoughts without reacting to them.** People who become really good at mindfulness can acknowledge a feeling without having symptoms of anxiety. For example, they might say to themselves, "I'm feeling worried about seeing my friend tomorrow since we had an argument today." They learn to let that feeling flow into and out of their brains and return their attention to what is happening right now. This trains their brains to have feelings and thoughts without being controlled by them.

It's very difficult for your brain to continue to be worried if you keep returning your focus to the present moment and paying attention only to what is happening right now. Being mindful is the opposite of being anxious, and your brain can't do both at the same time very well. Anxiety will sometimes simply give up. But like anything worthwhile, mindfulness takes practice. At first, it might feel very difficult to focus your thinking on the present. That's normal! But focusing on the present gets easier the more you practice. After a few weeks of practicing mindfulness for a few minutes every day, many people report that they feel better about themselves and feel less anxiety.

## How Can You Practice Mindfulness?

There are lots of ways to practice mindfulness. You can even do it during breakfast. Try noticing your cereal, how it looks in the bowl, how the cold milk feels in your mouth, and what smells are in the room. That's mindfulness! Here are some other ways to practice:

- yoga
- mindfulness apps (you will need to ask an adult to help you choose or buy a good one)
- mindful walking (notice how it feels to walk and the sights, sounds, and smells around you)
- mindful words (pick a soothing word—maybe peace or sunshine—and repeat it each time you breathe in and out, for about a minute)

## Deep Breathing

Deep breathing is a common mindfulness practice. And breathing slowly and deeply can help stop your amygdala from taking control.

Your amygdala only understands simple things (breathing fast = danger; breathing slow = no danger), so send it a simple message. Tell your amygdala that you are not in danger by breathing deeply and calmly. Try to imagine you are blowing bubbles. You can also count to five as you inhale, hold it for a moment, then count to five as you exhale. Another way to practice deep breathing is to lie down and place a lightweight object (like a small stuffed animal) on your stomach. Then make the object go up and down with each slow breath. Deep breathing sends "calm-down" messages in your brain, helps you use some physical activity to burn off anxiety energy, and exercises the parts of your brain that are responsible for calming you.

Deep breathing gets recommended to kids a lot. At first, it may not feel like it helps when you're feeling anxiety. But if you practice it often, including at times when you are not feeling anxiety, you'll get better and better at using it when you *are* feeling anxiety.

## Downtime

Anxiety is exhausting. Being busy all the time and running from one activity or class to the next can also be tiring and might make you feel more stressed and anxious. Sometimes when people get overwhelmed with all the things they have to do, they feel their muscles tense up or their stomach hurt. And you know that those can be symptoms of anxiety. *Downtime* is a word that means relaxing or doing something just for fun. But some popular downtime activities have powerful effects. Here are some ways downtime can help anxiety.

**Laughing produces brain messages that help you feel happier and less worried.** Good downtime activities can be things that make you laugh, like watching a funny movie or reading a book of jokes.

**Hugging or spending time with a loved one or pet can produce brain messages that help you feel happy and calm.** When you have some downtime, you might spend it with someone you love—cooking a meal or going outside together. Or you might play or cuddle with a pet.

**After doing something you enjoy, you might feel less anxiety for a while.** When you work on something you really like—building a model, writing a story, or playing a favorite sport—your brain can become very focused on that activity. It makes messages that help you stay focused. It also doesn't have as much time to send messages about worries, so you feel less anxiety.

It's good to have downtime in your life. Weekends, before bed, or right after school can be great times to do something you enjoy. If you need to, you can set a timer to remind you when downtime is over so that you don't forget to do your homework or take care of other responsibilities.

# Finding Activities for Downtime

Some kids can name a lot of things they enjoy doing. Other kids have a harder time thinking of something. They may have felt anxiety for so long that it's difficult to remember what they feel calm and happy doing. You might need to **brainstorm** activities that you used to like a lot and that might take your mind off your worries. Here are some ideas and questions to get you started.

- Ask family or friends what they remember you enjoying in the past. They might also have suggestions for new things to try.

- Look at some old pictures of yourself. What were you doing? Who were you with? You might find activities and friends you want to make time for.

- What's the best part of your day? You might be able to turn it into a happy hobby. If being with your parents is the best thing, maybe you can help cook dinner to spend more time with them. If you feel glad when your class gets to read silently, maybe you'd like to read more at home.

- What did you like doing when you were very young? Sometimes those activities can be very calming even though you are older now. Coloring is a great example. There are printable coloring pages as well as coloring books for older kids and adults. (Yes, even adults like coloring. Why? It's relaxing!)

- What do you see other people doing that you think looks fun? Maybe a relative can teach you how to knit, make birdhouses, fix things, or bake. Maybe you like the music someone listens to and want to hear more of it. Maybe you can help garden or do things around the house.

After thinking about these questions, come up with one or two downtime activities you can try right away. It can also be helpful to write your answers to these questions in a notebook or journal. That way, you can come back to your brainstorm when you are looking for more downtime activities.

## Brainstorm:

Thinking of ideas or solutions.

**A word about screen time:** Lots of people like to go online, watch TV, use social media, or play video games during downtime. You might be one of them. And some kids with anxiety find that time on screens does exactly what they want during downtime—it focuses their brain on something else so they can forget about worrying for a while. But other kids may get more anxious from playing a lot of video games or just being on screens too much. Social media can be a good way to connect with friends and family, but some kids feel bad about themselves or worry after using it that they are missing out on something. Often kids and parents disagree about how much screen time is okay. If playing video games, watching videos or TV, or connecting with friends online helps you, tell your parents that. Maybe you can work together to come up with a plan that will work for you and your parents. For example, if you find one or two other things that also help you feel calm (like playing music or drawing), maybe you can use some downtime for screens and some for your other activity.

# What You Can Do When You Feel Anxiety

*When I am worried, adults tell me to try not to think about it. But that just makes me worry more!*

You probably already know that trying not to worry doesn't work. If you've ever been told "Don't eat any more cookies," you might have noticed that suddenly the only thing you can think about is having another cookie! Anxiety is similar. Being told "Don't worry about it" only makes the worry thought bigger. When you feel anxiety, your brain is sending messages to focus only on the danger (or imagined danger). Anxiety narrows what you can focus on. It zooms you in. This makes it very hard to pay attention to anything outside your brain and body.

# Anxiety is an attention hog!

Focusing only on the worry would make sense if you needed to handle a real danger (like needing to escape a ferocious lion). That would definitely not be the time to think about other things, like which movie you want to see this weekend. But when you are actually safe, being zoomed in causes problems. It makes it really difficult to pay attention to your teacher, have fun with your friends, or do much of anything other than worry. And you probably *need* to focus on other things, like schoolwork, the dinner table conversation your family is having, or what your choir director is telling you to practice this week. What you need are ways to make your brain think about things that are outside of you.

A few things happen when you focus on things outside of yourself.

**You confuse your brain (in a good way).** You send brain messages that there are other things besides your worry to pay attention to.

**You tell your brain that there isn't any danger.** If you are paying attention to multiple things, your brain can only conclude that there must not be a real danger. It literally cannot compute that there could be a major danger and also lots of other interesting things to focus on. So it assumes there is nothing to worry about, and it starts to calm down.

**You tell anxiety to give up.** If it can't get all the attention, then anxiety often doesn't even want to stick around.

Here are some ideas for how to focus on other things or confuse your brain (in a good way).

## Name Anxiety and Talk Back to It

By giving your anxiety a name, you make it something separate from yourself. This can help remind you that your worry—for example, about going to a party—doesn't mean that something is wrong with you. Instead, anxiety has become a separate thing that you can talk back to and tell to take a hike. "I think Anxiety has me worried about this party. Luckily, I know my friend will be there and there will be cake. Anxiety doesn't really know much about parties." You can name your anxiety anything you want: Bob, the Attention Hog, or just simply Anxiety.

## Is It Anxiety or Excitement?

Excitement can feel a lot like anxiety—your heart rate goes up, you might breathe faster, and you may feel jittery or find it hard to concentrate. If you feel those symptoms before something you were looking forward to (a fun trip, seeing friends after a summer apart, starting middle school) or before a performance (a big game, a test, giving a speech in class), you might actually be feeling excitement. It can be hard to know for sure since anxiety and excitement cause similar reactions in your body. You could try using one of your calming strategies, but it may actually be easier to tell yourself you are feeling excited. For example, if you wake up on the last day of school feeling nervous about the end-of-the-year party that afternoon, say out loud, "I'm so excited about the party!" This can help you change how you think about your symptoms and make it easier to focus on the positive parts of your day.

## Write Down Your Schedule

Writing requires you to slow down and focus on what you are doing right now. Writing down your schedule for the day can also help you feel prepared and like you know what to expect. When there is less unknown, there is less to feel anxiety about.

## Send Anxiety Out of Your Body

Take a deep breath and notice your body. On the next breath, imagine you are gathering all your feelings of anxiety in one place (your lungs, your tight fist, or even your scrunched toes). When you exhale, blow the anxiety out of your lungs or open your fists or toes to send the anxiety out of your body. You can also try tensing and relaxing each part of your body. This is sometimes called "progressive relaxation." Lie down on your back. Starting with your head, squeeze your mouth and eyes like you just tasted a sour lemon. Then, relax those muscles. Move on to your shoulders, arms, stomach, and legs—tightening and then relaxing each group of muscles.

## Deep Breathing

Remember reading about deep breathing on page 56? If you've practiced it in times when you feel calm, you'll be more ready to use it in times when you feel anxiety. To lower anxiety in the moment, try breathing in as you count to five (slowly!) and then breathing out as you count to five. Repeat a few times.

## Partner Breathing

It can help to work on deep breathing with a trusted adult. This strategy is also useful if you are feeling a lot of anxiety and are having a hard time using your other calming strategies. A trusted adult who is calm can breathe with you to help you relax and slow your breathing. Sit across from your partner and look into their eyes. If this makes you uncomfortable, you can look at their belly. Start breathing deeply, looking at your adult model. Your breathing might sync up with your adult partner's or it might not.

## Make Anxiety Funny

Change the thing you are afraid of into something silly or funny. If you are worried to get into a car because there could be an accident, you might imagine all the cars covered in spongy marshmallows to cushion them.

## Make a Calming Toolkit

Think about each of your senses and what items might help you focus on that sense. Get a shoebox and put these items inside. For example, you could include mints to suck on (taste), lavender or a scratch-and-sniff sticker to smell (scent), a photo of your pet or family to look at (sight), and a smooth stone or piece of satin fabric to feel (touch). When you are experiencing symptoms of anxiety, you can open the box and taste, smell, look at, and feel the things you like. This moves your focus from anxiety to your environment.

## Get a Cold Drink

Get a cold (or warm!) drink, or even a popsicle. The temperature change brings your focus to your senses of touch and taste and can be a quick way to disrupt anxiety.

## Name the Things Around You

Say or think the names of regular things that are in the space around you ("My bed, the window, the books." "The car door, an old snack wrapper, the road."). Or name all the things you can see that are a certain color.

## 5-4-3-2-1

This is a countdown that uses your senses. You can use this in the moment when you're feeling anxiety. Start by naming five things you can see, five things you can hear, five things you can feel or touch, five things you can smell, and five things you can taste. Then start over and name four things for each sense. Continue until you get down to one. To make it most effective, see if you can avoid repeating any items in your list (but it's okay if you do repeat—you might only taste one or two things!).

## What's That Smell?

Take a deep sniff and figure out everything you can smell. You can also intentionally smell something that is relaxing to you. Many people find the scent of lavender or lemon to be calming.

# How to Plan for Anxiety

There may be something you avoid because you feel anxiety about it. A small fear (falling off your bike) may have already grown into a much bigger fear (riding your bike at all), and just using a calming strategy isn't enough. Bigger fears sometimes need to be worked on in stages, not all at once. Just like your brain can fall for the trick of imagined danger, it can also be trained to remember that you are okay. You might want to make a plan for anxiety if there is a fear you *really want* to overcome. Making a plan takes a bigger anxiety and breaks it down into smaller, more manageable parts. It takes time, but breaking it down makes it more likely that you will reach your goal of overcoming the fear.

Here's how to make a plan to overcome anxiety:

1. **Write down the steps you will take.** Make a list of steps you will take toward overcoming your fear. (A trusted adult can help with this.) Your list might be only a couple steps, or it might be longer. What's important is to have as many steps as you think you need. The first step should be something you think would be uncomfortable to do, but not impossible. The middle steps should be more and more challenging—like bigger and bigger boss battles in a video game—so that when you get to the last step, it's only a little bit harder than the step right before it. (But right now, at the beginning, the last step probably feels impossible. That's okay.)

2. **Decide how you will calm yourself while you practice each step.** Deep breathing or naming all the things around you that are a certain color can be good ways to remind your brain you are safe as you try each step. For more ideas, take a look at the anxiety-taming strategies starting on page 62.

3. **Decide how you will reward yourself.** Overcoming anxiety is hard work, and you deserve a reward. Perhaps you can do something fun with a friend, or maybe you'll get to pick which movie your family watches this weekend. Will you reward yourself when you complete each step or wait until the very end?

4. **Start with your first step.** Keep repeating it until it becomes easy. Maybe you'll work on it every day or every week—whatever you and your trusted adult decide.

5. **Move on to the next step.** Work through your steps in order, repeating whichever one you are on until it feels easy or comfortable. Then move on to the next step in your list. You might spend more time on some steps than others, and some lists may take weeks of practice to get through. That's okay! Listen to yourself and don't move on until you are ready.

6. **Keep going until you can do the final step with very little worry.** Congratulations! You have conquered your fear! You can make a new plan for each of the fears you want to overcome.

## My Anxiety Plan

My goal: Ride my bike without worrying about crashing.

My calming strategies: Deep breathing and talking back to The Worrier.

How I'll reward myself: Game night!

Step 1: Stand next to my bike for one minute.

Step 2: Sit on my bike without moving for one minute.

Step 3: Ride my bike in front of the house with Dad nearby.

Final step: Take a bike ride in the park.

Think about a fear you want to overcome and make a plan in a notebook or journal using the steps above.

Try one or two of the strategies you learned in this chapter for a while to see if they work well for you. If a strategy doesn't work, you might need to practice it a few more times. If it's still not helping, it's okay to move on and try something else. There are many ways to manage anxiety and it's best to use whatever strategies work for you.

# Therapy

Some people can manage anxiety using the calming tools and other ideas that we discussed in chapter 4. Many people with anxiety also decide to go to **therapy**. Therapy is a regular appointment—like a class—where you get to work on ways to train your brain to manage anxiety. Your parents might decide it would be helpful for you, or a doctor might recommend it. (Therapy can be expensive. You can ask your school counselor or your pediatrician if they know about low-cost or free resources that can help you.) Therapy might sound a bit like going to the doctor, and in some ways it is. But you don't go to therapy just once to fix a problem. This chapter will give you answers to some common questions kids ask about therapy.

## Therapy:

Treatment to relieve a problem or help with healing. If you have an infection, your doctor might prescribe antibiotic therapy to treat it. If you have an injured arm, you might do muscle stretches as physical therapy to get back to full strength. If you have anxiety, you might meet with a counselor for psychotherapy to help you learn to manage anxiety.

# Who Are Therapists?

When you go to therapy, the person who helps you is a therapist. You might also hear them called a counselor. A therapist has gone to college and then gone to graduate school (*more* college) to learn about how brains work and how to help people solve all kinds of problems. A person who works with kids in therapy may be a psychologist or a psychiatrist—in which case, they probably introduce themselves as Dr. So-and-So. Other therapists may have you call them Mr. or Ms. like your teachers do, or they might just have you use their first name. The important thing to remember is that all therapists know lots of ways to manage anxiety.

# What Makes a Therapist?

There are several kinds of professionals who can provide therapy.

A **counselor** or **therapist** has a master's degree, usually in childhood development, counseling, family therapy, or social work. This takes four years of college, two to three years of graduate school, and often some specialized training.

A **psychologist** has a Ph.D. or a Psy.D., which are doctorate-level degrees in psychology. This takes four years of college and then four to eight years of graduate school.

A **psychiatrist** has an M.D., or a medical doctor degree. This takes four years of college, four years of medical school, and then about four years of specialized training. Because psychiatrists are medical doctors, they can prescribe medication.

You may see one of these kinds of professionals for therapy, or you may end up seeing a combination of people as part of a therapy team.

# Finding a Good Fit

Have you ever had a teacher you really liked and felt comfortable with? How about a teacher you didn't like very much? Wouldn't it be cool if you could meet several teachers at the beginning of the year and decide which one you wanted? You don't usually get to choose your teachers, but this is often how finding a therapist works. It's important to find a therapist you are comfortable talking to and solving problems with, and it's okay to try out several therapists until you find the right one. (Or your parents or guardians might talk to several therapists before picking one for you.) You'll probably see your therapist for at least a few months, and you'll practice a lot of strategies together, so picking the right person is important.

## What Happens in the Therapist's Office?

You might go to therapy at the clinic you go to for your regular doctor's visits, or you might go to a new clinic. Some therapists rent an office in a building with lots of other therapists (or other medical offices), and others might have an office in their house. It's also possible you won't go anywhere at all, but instead have video appointments.

The therapist's office may have a waiting room. When you are waiting for your appointment, you might see other people in the waiting room. Some kids wonder if this means other people will know why they are going to therapy. But nobody except you, your parents, and the therapist knows why you are there. There are many, *many* reasons people seek out therapy. Anxiety is only one of them. (And hey, that person in the waiting room is probably ALSO there for therapy!)

You might check in with a receptionist, or your therapist's office may have a little button to push (or bell to ring) so that the therapist knows you have arrived. Usually the therapist's door is closed to keep their appointments private, so they aren't able to see that their next patient is in the waiting room. The button turns on a light inside the office, and it stays lit until the therapist turns it off. So once you've pushed it, you can be sure your therapist knows you are there. The therapist will finish up their work and then come out to greet you.

The inside of the therapist's office may have some things you've seen in other offices, like a desk, chairs, and a computer.

But it may also have things you don't find in many other offices:

- some toys or fidgets (things to fiddle with)
- a couch
- a white-noise machine (This is a little box that makes a steady whoosh sound and makes it very hard for anyone outside the office to hear what is being talked about inside the office. This helps the things you talk about with your therapist stay private.)

Therapists like their offices to feel comfortable. They want it to be a place where you feel safe and relaxed. It is very normal to feel symptoms of anxiety the first time you go to a therapist. It's even normal for your parents to feel anxious. After all, this is a new thing for your family.

The first time you talk to a therapist (often called a therapy "session"), an adult will probably go with you. You'll most likely talk to the therapist together. The therapist may tell you a little bit about how she helps kids with anxiety. Mostly, she will want to get to know you. She may ask questions about your school, your home, and what things you like to do. She may also take notes while you talk. This is so she can look back to remember important things about you and keep track of what strategies the two of you are working on.

**"Why do psychologists ask, 'Do you know why you're here today?' I never know what to say!"**

Here's a translation for that grown-up garble: "I'm wondering if you already understand anxiety and therapy or if it would be helpful for me to explain those things now. And I'm wondering if *you* want to try therapy or if you are just here because someone made you come."

This is not a test. Sometimes kids and parents haven't talked about why they are going to a therapist's office. Other kids have talked about it a lot with their caregivers or doctor. But the therapist doesn't know, so she asks this question to find out if she should help by explaining things. It's okay to answer honestly, and it doesn't mean you are in trouble. There is no right or wrong answer.

Then, the therapist may ask you to wait outside the room while she talks to the adult you came with. Or she may talk with just you.

## What Are Adults Talking About in There?

The therapist may want to get a little more information about any illnesses you've had in the past, or any other times you've been to therapy. She may want to ask your parents about why *they* think therapy might be helpful for you. And she may be telling them that they will have to do parent homework!

The therapist will make a plan with you and your parents about how often you'll come to therapy appointments and what you'll do in them. Here are some questions you might want to ask your therapist:

- Will an adult come into the office with me each time, or will they wait in the waiting room?
- What kinds of things do you do to help kids manage anxiety?
- Will I have things to practice in between therapy sessions?
- How long will each therapy appointment last?
- How often will I come here?
- When will I be done with therapy?
- Do other kids come here? Will they know I come here?

You might have some other questions about therapy too. It can help to write down a list of all the questions you want to ask your therapist before your first appointment. Having a list can help you remember what you want to ask so you don't forget anything important.

## What Happens in Therapy?

You'll most likely go to therapy on a regular schedule, just like other classes you take. You may go every Tuesday, or you may go once per month. Each appointment will last the same amount of time—usually between 30 minutes and an hour. Therapy is different from a lot of the other classes you take because you're the only student.

Usually therapy is done one-on-one, but sometimes therapists hold classes for a small group of kids who are all working on similar things.

The therapist usually starts by checking in to see how you are doing. He might ask how school is, what friends you've seen lately, or about anything fun that has happened since you last met.

After checking in, what happens next depends on the therapist. But most likely, he will ask you something about anxiety. Maybe it will be a question about specific times when you felt anxiety, or how often you felt it. He may also ask what you did or what strategies you tried. This is not a test. There is no right or wrong answer. Talking to the therapist about how you feel and what you do with those feelings gives him information to decide what might help you most.

The therapist may suggest a new strategy for you to try. He may give you an assignment to practice the strategy between your therapy sessions. Sometimes the assignment may seem easy, and sometimes it may seem difficult or uncomfortable. It's good to know that you are in control. You can tell the therapist if you don't think a strategy will work or if you don't want to try it. It's also good to have an open mind and be willing to try things out and see what happens. The therapist, and your parents, do not want you to be in any danger. If they make a suggestion to try a strategy, it is safe to try it, even if (for now) you feel anxiety about it. You can also talk to a parent, foster parent, or other trusted adult about the strategy and see what they think.

## Cognitive Behavioral Therapy

There are many kinds of therapy. Most therapy includes talking about your experiences and feelings. Cognitive behavioral therapy (CBT) is the most common and most effective type of therapy for anxiety. In CBT, you learn ways to change your thinking so you can take control of anxiety. In your therapy sessions, you'll learn ways to do this (breathing exercises and talking back to anxiety are two examples) and you'll practice these strategies with your therapist. You may get an assignment to try what you learned at home, and then report how it worked at your next appointment.

Exposure and response prevention therapy (ERP) is a type of CBT that is done with a therapist and is often used with people who have obsessive-compulsive disorder. ERP works a lot like the plan for anxiety you read about in chapter 4. You gradually expose yourself to a thing (or situation) that makes you feel anxiety and learn to tolerate the anxious feelings until they decrease or go away. Anxiety isn't good at sticking around for a long time. If you wait it out, it will often go away on its own. Think of it like getting used to the loud noises that come with fireworks. The first few fireworks seem extremely loud and even frightening. But as you keep watching them, you get used to the sound and you feel less shocked when you hear one. When you do ERP with a therapist, you'll make an **exposure** plan and practice one step at a time.

**Exposure:**

To expose or be in contact with something. If you cut open a watermelon, you expose the red fruit and the seeds. If you go to a museum, you are exposing yourself to art.

## How Long Will I Go to Therapy?

It depends on the *goal* of therapy—what problem are you and your therapist trying to solve? Maybe you will be focusing on one specific thing, like talking to new people. Or maybe you'll be working on several strategies that you can use any time you become anxious. Either way, you'll need to learn step by step and practice what you learn. It takes time to get really good at anything new. So therapy takes a while.

When therapy ends can depend on a number of things: what the goal of therapy was and whether it has been met, whether you and your parents feel like therapy with this therapist is working, how motivated you are to continue doing therapy work, the cost of therapy, and other factors. In an ideal situation where you have gotten a lot of help from the therapist, eventually he and your parents may decide it's a good time to end or take a break. This is a happy event—you've made a lot of progress toward taking control of your anxiety! You should feel happy and proud. You might also feel a little sad that you won't see your therapist anymore or nervous about being "on your own." Those are all normal feelings, especially since kids and adults can build very strong relationships with their therapists. After therapy ends, you should keep using the strategies you learned in therapy that help you.

Most kids go to therapy for at least 10 to 12 sessions. Some kids may take a break after those sessions. Other kids may feel better if they keep going to therapy for a longer time. When they decide (with their parents and therapist) to end therapy, they may never need it again. Or they might go back when they are older or if it feels like anxiety is taking control again.

# 6 How Anxiety Works in Your Brain (and How Medication Can Help)

Your brain makes chemical messages called **neurotransmitters**. There are dozens of types of these messages. Serotonin is a type of brain message about mood. When you're feeling happy, your brain is sending and receiving serotonin messages. When you are feeling anxious, you probably aren't getting enough of those messages. But if you know calming strategies and some other ways to help send out more serotonin messages, you can help your brain send and receive them. Those messages tell all the parts of your brain that everything is okay and they can stop freaking out now. You may have heard of other neurotransmitters, like dopamine (which your brain sends when you are doing something pleasurable, and which helps you learn, remember, and focus) and adrenaline (which is sent when you are stressed or scared and gives you a burst of energy to engage in fight-or-flight behaviors).

## Neurotransmitter:

A chemical message in your brain.

## How Brain Messages Get Delivered

Neurotransmitter messages such as serotonin leave one neuron and jump over space to another neuron, where the message is received. (This is kind of like how a mail carrier picks up mail from your mailbox and delivers it to someone else's house.) When messages don't make it all the way to the second neuron or stay too long in the space between neurons, they get removed from your body—the letter gets lost in the mail.

> **Fact!** Did you know that serotonin isn't just made in your brain? It's also made in your stomach! Sometimes, if you have diarrhea, it's because your body thinks you ate something dangerous and sends extra serotonin messages to get that food out of there. Gross, yet fascinating.

We know that sometimes brains don't get the message that everything is okay. Even if you *know* you want to stop worrying, if you don't have enough serotonin, the message to stop being worried doesn't always get through to your hypothalamus and amygdala. (Remember them from chapter 2?) If you don't have the right amount of serotonin, you might worry a lot.

Humans need enough serotonin to deliver important mood messages in our brains. So, how do you make sure you have enough serotonin? Can you just grab a serotonin bar for a snack and replenish your neurotransmitter levels?

If only it were that easy . . .

Actually, you make serotonin in your body. Humans don't have a lot of control over how our bodies do this. It's mostly genetic (see Heredity on page 22), which means it runs in families. But we do know some things that can encourage the body to make more serotonin. And when your brain has the right amount of serotonin, it is easier to tell anxiety to stop and that everything is okay.

## How to Make Serotonin

There are a few ways you can encourage your body to make more serotonin.

**Bright light.** Getting outside into the sunshine tells your brain to make serotonin. Try to spend at least 10 to 15 minutes outdoors each day. Even if it's a cloudy day, the outdoor light is bright enough to help. In places where the weather makes it very difficult to be outdoors or there are only a few hours of light per day, some people use a light therapy box to help them get enough bright light.

**Food.** Eating foods with tryptophan in them can help your body make serotonin. Tryptophan is actually an ingredient in serotonin. It's found in foods like eggs, cheese, nuts, red meat, and turkey. Add some carbohydrates (like bread) to boost your tryptophan snack! Try whole wheat bread with turkey; a few crackers with cheese; or slices of banana topped with almond butter.

And the big one . . .

**Exercise.** When you exercise, you tell your brain to make more serotonin and other important neurotransmitters. Exercise is basically the solution to everything.

Did you notice that some of the things that help you make serotonin are also things that help lower anxiety (see chapter 4)? This is not a coincidence. The physical things you do help change your brain messages, or brain chemistry.

For some people, a serotonin boost from these things is enough to help them manage anxiety. And everyone should get exercise, eat healthy foods, and get outdoors in the sunlight because these things are important for A LOT of brain functions as well as overall health. But for some people, even going for a daily, outdoor, post-turkey-sandwich jog doesn't boost their serotonin levels enough.

# Medication for Anxiety

Another tool for managing anxiety is medication, though not every kid with anxiety takes medication. If your doctor and parents have talked about this with you, you might have heard about the effects of anxiety medicine—for example, that you'll worry less. But often, kids and parents don't have more information than that. So you may not have heard the whole story about what anxiety medication does—and doesn't do—in your body.

It's good to understand what medications do in your body. (**Bonus!** After you learn this, you can teach the adults in your life, because often *they* don't even know how these medications work.)

The most commonly prescribed type of medications for anxiety are Selective Serotonin Reuptake Inhibitors (or just say the initials, SSRI). They're often called antidepressants because they can also be used to treat depression (a condition where a person may feel sad, lack energy, and not enjoy the things they used to). There are a lot of SSRIs. They usually come in small pills you swallow or in a liquid you can drink. Though all SSRIs work in basically the same way, each is made a little bit differently. A person may find that one SSRI works better for them than another SSRI. Everyone is different!

Sometimes it can take trial and error to figure out which medication works best for you. That means you might have to try a few, one at a time, to find out which fits you best.

## How SSRIs Work

You may be prescribed an SSRI because your doctor believes that having more serotonin in your brain will help you manage anxiety. Even though we can help our bodies make serotonin naturally, we can't totally control how much we make or what happens after we make it. Normally, once a serotonin message has been delivered, it gets "reabsorbed" or disposed of by the body—like putting the mail in the recycling bin after you read it. But some people's brains recycle the messages before they get delivered, throwing them away before they can be read. Since we can't simply get ourselves a fresh batch of serotonin, scientists figured out another option: stop the serotonin you *do* have from being dumped into the recycling bin so soon. That way, it will stay in your brain longer and can deliver important mood messages.

How does your doctor know you don't have enough serotonin? Your doctor asks questions about your symptoms and listens to your answers and then determines that it is likely you have low serotonin.

How does an SSRI do this? The SSRI gets in the way of the recycling bin. Your brain will still dispose of, or reuptake, some of the serotonin. Just not as much. And for you, and millions of people, that makes all the difference in the world. It means more serotonin neurotransmitters are available in your brain to deliver important messages that help you feel less anxiety.

# What Happens When You Take an SSRI

You'll take an SSRI every day, and for a while, it may seem like nothing is happening. Within a few weeks, however, you (or your parents) may notice changes:

- Some things that used to make you very anxious don't seem quite so bad anymore.
- It's easier to focus on the things you like to do.
- You may not feel the need to ask over and over again if something will be okay.
- You may not worry so much about what other people are thinking about you.
- You may feel less tired.
- You may suddenly start doing (safe) things you used to be afraid of.
- You may feel fewer symptoms of anxiety.

" My family goes camping every year. One year, after I had just started taking an SSRI, I climbed on top of a huge tree stump. I was just having fun, but my parents were in shock—I had always been too afraid to climb them before. "

Why are these things changing?

When you take an SSRI, the medication helps keep the serotonin messages in your brain longer, so they can get where they need to go. This means that your smart prefrontal cortex can deliver messages to your amygdala that things are okay, that you can handle this, and that it is fine to calm down now. The medication gives you the power to be in charge and tell anxiety to back off!

## What Does NOT Happen When You Take an SSRI

When you take an SSRI, it has no power to change your personality. It doesn't even have the power to make you stop worrying. Your amygdala is in charge of worrying and—as we've established—it is awesome at its job. An SSRI simply stops your brain from throwing away so much serotonin. So when you and your prefrontal cortex want to send a message saying to chill out or stop worrying about something, an SSRI makes sure that *the message gets through.*

That's all an SSRI is.

You will still be creative, or athletic, or loving, or funny, or whatever makes you, you. You'll even still have worries. You'll just be in better control of how much you worry and how you want to handle the situation. *You* get to be in control, not anxiety! And over time, that will make some things you used to worry about—school, homework, planes, spiders, lions in the park—less worrisome. Because now you'll tell your amygdala, "Thanks, but I've got this," and your amygdala will happily get the message.

## What It Feels Like to Take Anxiety Medication

You might be wondering what it feels like when you're taking medication for anxiety. Many kids say that it doesn't feel like anything or that it makes them feel calmer and happier because they are able to worry less. Medication for anxiety does not hurt and does not change your personality.

Only a medical doctor can prescribe medication. Your doctor will probably start you with a low dose (amount) of medication. Starting with a small amount helps your doctor make sure that you don't have unwanted side effects from the medication. You'll talk with your doctor and/or therapist and gradually increase the dose until you get to a point where you, your parents, and your doctor agree that the medication is helping your anxiety. Needing to increase your dose doesn't mean you're doing something wrong.

Every person is different, and the only way to tell how much medication a person needs is to try higher doses, little by little. As you grow and your brain changes, you may need to change your dose again. That's okay too.

## Side Effects of Anxiety Medications

Side effects are unpleasant things that happen alongside the good things a medication does. Some people will have no side effects. Others will. A common side effect of SSRIs is a stomachache. Other side effects include headaches, trouble sleeping, or a dry mouth. Usually the side effects from SSRIs are not too bad, and they often go away after a few weeks, once your body gets used to the medication. If they don't go away after a few weeks, or if the side effects are too much to live with, talk to your parents and doctor. You should also talk to them if you feel something new or unpleasant but don't know if it's a side effect, even if you've been on the SSRI for quite a while. Your doctor may suggest a different dose or a different SSRI. It can take some time to get things just right.

## How Long to Take Anxiety Medication

The medications you may have taken before (like antibiotics for an infection) are usually only for a few days. Medication for anxiety is taken for much longer. It can take a few weeks just to feel like an SSRI has started working. Once the medication is working well and you are feeling less anxiety, you and your therapist and family will want to practice other strategies for managing anxiety and get really good at them. (These strategies can be easier to practice when you have medication to help!) You have to take SSRIs every day for them to work. Most kids using an SSRI will take it for at least several months. Some kids will stop taking an SSRI after some months or years. Others will stay on their medication for longer. It just depends on what works for you. If you want to stop taking an SSRI, talk to your therapist or doctor so that they can help you gradually lower the dose. You should never stop taking an SSRI on your own.

# PART 3

## Talking About Anxiety

# 7

# Self-Advocacy

When you were younger, you probably had an adult explain to other adults what you needed. Maybe your mom explained to a teacher that you get nervous about being called on in school. Or perhaps the principal explained to your gym teacher that you feel less anxious and more able to participate if you know ahead of time what you'll be doing in class. And then the adults worked out a plan to help you manage your anxiety. An adult **advocated** for you by explaining what you needed in order to be successful.

## Advocate:

(AD-vo-kate). To support or champion another person's cause or needs. To self-advocate means to stand up for your own needs. As a noun, an advocate (AD-vo-ket) is a person who stands up for others' needs. A self-advocate is a person who stands up for their own needs.

As you get older, it's important to be able to advocate for yourself. Being a self-advocate means understanding the things that you are good at and that you like as well as the things that are more difficult for you. When you self-advocate, you are not complaining or asking to get out of doing something. You are explaining the reason something is difficult for you and asking for help (also called an accommodation) to make it possible for you to do it. Self-advocacy gets you the help you need from other people. If you are self-advocating about anxiety, it works best if you also explain to the person that you are working on managing your anxiety. Together, you can work out an **accommodation** to help you. An accommodation may be temporary, or it may last a long time. In either case, the goal of the accommodation is to help you get better and better at managing anxiety.

## Accommodation:

An adjustment or adaptation to fit a specific person's needs.

# When to Self-Advocate

You can self-advocate any time—at home, in a class, or even when you are visiting someone else's home. And you can explain your needs to adults or to other kids. Any time you need help, it is okay to ask for it! But when you are asking another person to help you by making a change or accommodation that is big or that may last a long time, getting the timing right can make a positive difference. To get what you need, it's best if you can talk to the person when you are feeling relatively unworried *and* when the other person is not too busy to really listen.

Not-so-good times to self-advocate are when the other person is in a hurry, when they need to pay attention to others, or after plans have already been finalized. Times when you probably want to wait include:

- Right in the middle of class when your teacher is teaching or just as your soccer coach puts you in to play

- In the morning when your parent is scrambling to get everyone out the door

- Right when you arrive at your cousin's house

- During theater practice or right when the curtain is about to open

- When your friend has exciting news to share with you or when there are lots of other kids around

Better times to self-advocate are when things are quiet, the other person can focus on you, and there is still time to make changes to plans. Some good times to self-advocate are:

- Before or after school or practice, so your teacher or coach isn't distracted by other students

- At dinner, on the weekend, or another time when your parent isn't in a hurry

- Before you go to your cousin's house, or during a quiet moment while you are visiting

- Before or after practice, or as far ahead of a performance as possible, so your theater or music director has time to make a change

- When you and your friend are alone and have time to talk (in-person is usually better than texting)

At first, you might only think about self-advocating when you're "in the moment" and feeling anxiety about something. It's okay to talk to an adult or a friend in that moment. However, they may be unable to give you their full attention and you may have a hard time focusing on what you need to say. It can be better to simply ask to talk later about a problem you are having. You might also try writing down what you want to talk to them about so that you'll remember to bring it up at a better time. It's best if you can talk with the person at a time when you both feel calm and won't be distracted.

Sometimes, particularly at school, a meeting about accommodations needs to be official, with your parents and teachers all in the room. But other times, you can solve small problems or ask for an accommodation on your own. It can help to talk with a parent first to decide how best to handle asking for help at school.

# How to Self-Advocate

Being a self-advocate means communicating what you need to another person—sitting down to have a chat or a meeting. You might feel anxious at the thought of meeting with someone to talk about anxiety. That's understandable! There are some things you can do to help yourself self-advocate and feel less anxious during a meeting or conversation.

**Organize and write down your thoughts before you meet.** Write down the problem or the situation that is causing your anxiety, and how you feel when it happens. If you have ideas for possible accommodations or solutions, write those down too. Bring what you wrote to the meeting to help you remember all your thoughts.

**Practice what you'll say.** Just like practicing for a presentation in class, practicing what you'll say in the meeting can help you feel more prepared and confident. An older sibling or a parent might be willing to play the role of the person you will be talking to, or you can practice in front of a mirror.

**Bring some support.** You and the person who can help you should do most of the talking, but you might feel better if a parent, grandparent, best friend, or sibling is with you. Your support person can have the job of listening and helping you remember what was said later on. That way, even if you feel nervous and forget some of the conversation, you'll have someone who can help remind you later. If you can't bring another person with you, you can bring a notebook and take notes.

**Thank the person for meeting with you.** It's important to thank the person at the beginning of the conversation for making time to talk with you, especially if you've set up a special meeting time. It shows that you appreciate the person, and when people feel appreciated, they become more interested in helping. (It's always a good idea to thank the person at the end of the conversation too!)

**Use I-messages.** When you speak to someone about needing support or an accommodation, it can help to put your words in a certain order:

When _____ happens, I feel _____ .
It would help me if _____ .

(If you don't know what would help, just ask the adult to help you figure that out!) An I-message or I-statement is a way to assertively state your feelings and ask for what you need without blaming or attacking the other person.

**Be assertive.** When asking for an accommodation, sit or stand up straight and look at the person you are talking to. Eye contact is great, but if you feel uncomfortable, it is okay to look just to the side of the person's face. Make sure to speak clearly and loudly enough for the other person to hear you.

**Assertive:**
Having confident statements and behavior.

**Expect questions and new ideas.** The other person may want to know more about how you feel. You can their answer questions honestly. If you can't think of an answer, it's okay to say so or to ask if you can think about it for a while. The other person may also have new ideas about how they can help. This is great! You might decide right then that their idea will work, or you might ask if you can think about the idea and meet again in a few days.

**Write down the plan.** If you and the other person agree on an accommodation that can help you, write down what was decided. This way you can read the plan later to remind yourself about what will happen. Writing down the plan and sharing it with the person who will be helping you makes sure that you both have the same expectations.

After you've met and agreed on a certain accommodation or plan, you might check in after a few days or weeks to see how things are going. You can also ask for a new or different accommodation later if the first one isn't working.

You can plan to self-advocate about something that frequently worries you. The questions on page 106 can help you organize your thoughts. Bring your answers with you when you meet to talk about the issue.

## Examples of Self-Advocacy

**The problem:** Your friend has a pet dog and you feel anxious around dogs.

**The place:** Your friend's house.

**The thought:** "I hate dogs. I don't want to go near them."

**The person to talk to:** Your friend or the adult in the house.

**Good self-advocacy:** Before you go to your friend's house, try calling your friend or talking to her at school. (You could also ask your parent to speak to an adult at your friend's home.) You might say, "When a dog comes close to me, I feel like I want to run away. When I come to your house, it would help me start to get used to dogs if I could just look your dog from a distance for now." Your friend and their family want you to feel comfortable at their home. Most likely, they'll be able to find a way to accommodate you, and they'll be glad you asked.

That's okay, we can keep Boomer on a leash.

**The problem:** You feel anxiety every day because you might be called on in class.

**The place:** School.

**The thought:** "I don't like being called on in class."

**The person to talk to:** Your teacher.

**Good self-advocacy:** Ask your teacher to meet with you at a time when you can both focus on your conversation (before or after school or at lunch are good options). You might say, "When I'm called on in school, I feel very worried that I'm going to say something wrong. Could we make a plan to help me get used to it?" Your teacher wants you to be comfortable in class and to be able to focus on learning. She'll probably be glad you talked with her, and she may have great ideas that have worked for other students.

**The problem:** When you will be apart from your stepdad, you worry that he won't return.

**The place:** The car (or subway, or bus, or walking).

**The thought:** "I don't want you to drop me off. You have to stay."

**The person to talk to:** Your stepdad.

**Good self-advocacy:** When your stepdad isn't in a hurry—maybe on the ride home or on a Saturday morning with no plans—sit down for a talk. You might say, "When you drop me off and leave, I feel worried that you won't come back and I won't know what to do. Can you help me make a plan to feel less worried?" The adults who take care of you want to understand how you are feeling, and they want you to gain confidence being on your own. They'll probably be eager to help you figure out a solution!

What do you want to self-advocate about? Try answering as many of the following questions as you can, and then set up a time to talk with someone who can help.

- What is the problem?
- Where does it happen?
- What are the thoughts in your head?
- Who can you talk to?
- When is a good time to talk?
- What can you say? (Remember to use an I-message.)
- What ideas do you have for accommodations?

You can refer to your answers to these questions when you talk the person. And be sure to write down any plans you both agree to.

## Who (and How Much) to Tell About Your Anxiety

Some people in your life probably already know you have anxiety. Adults at home probably know, and if you've been diagnosed with an anxiety disorder, your doctor or therapist knows. Maybe your sibling or a grandparent knows about your experiences with anxiety, but maybe not. Should you tell them? What about your friends or your teachers? Who you tell about anxiety and how much you tell them depends on whether you think of anxiety as public or personal information.

Public information is stuff that is obvious to anyone who meets you and less obvious stuff that you feel okay with most people knowing. Here are examples of things lots of people feel comfortable being public:

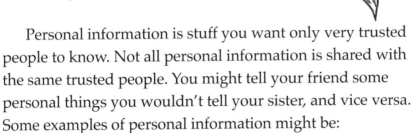

- What grade you're in
- Your pet's name
- Your favorite movie
- Your eye color

Personal information is stuff you want only very trusted people to know. Not all personal information is shared with the same trusted people. You might tell your friend some personal things you wouldn't tell your sister, and vice versa. Some examples of personal information might be:

- You sleep with a stuffed animal
- Your math test score
- Your crush
- That story about you playing in the bubble bath when you were a baby

Which category would you put anxiety into? What do your parents think? Everyone has their own comfort level about sharing that they have anxiety. Some people want it to be personal, and others want it to be public. It's important for you and your family to discuss how you will treat talking about anxiety to others. This helps you support each other and have confidence that none of you will unintentionally make the others feel uncomfortable. For example, you and your parents might decide that your teachers need to know about your anxiety so that they can help you manage it at school. But you might decide that the rest of your class does not need to know. You and your parents can tell your teachers that you'd like to keep this information private or personal. It's also okay to ask the people who are close to you not to share your personal information. Here's a way to self-advocate about this: "Grandma, I'd like to keep anxiety personal. Can you please not talk about it when we see your friends today?"

You can also change your mind about personal and public information. As you get older, you may become more (or less) comfortable with anxiety being public. As you get to know a new friend, you may eventually decide to tell them about your anxiety even if you didn't feel comfortable telling them at first.

## Translating Things Grown-Ups Say

Adults can say the strangest things. Here are some common things they say about anxiety, what they really mean, and how you can self-advocate when they say them.

**"Try not to think about it," or "Just don't worry about it."**

*When grown-ups say it:* Before school, before you get braces put on, before a test, when you are stuck on something a friend said that upset you.

*Why it doesn't work:* Any time you're told NOT to worry about something, you may worry about it more.

*Translation:* "The thing you are worried about is not actually unsafe and/or isn't actually happening right now. I feel confident you can handle it if/when it does happen."

*How you can respond:* "When I am told not to worry, I seem to worry more. Can you help me use one of my calming strategies instead?"

Remember that everyone feels anxiety sometimes. It's okay to feel that way. Try to stay busy doing something you like, take a moment to notice other things in the room, or use one of the other anxiety-taming strategies from chapter 4. Your brain will start to get the message that you're not in danger. Often, anxiety will give up after a little while.

## "There's nothing to worry about," or "There's nothing to be scared of."

*When grown-ups say it:* When you want reassurance that you'll be okay, when you are scared to do something or be alone, when you are worried something bad might happen to you or your family. Also when they are tired or just don't know how to help.

*Why it doesn't work:* Your amygdala believes there is something to worry about, and it's taking control.

*Translation:* "My job as the adult is to make sure you are safe, and I am confident you are safe right now."

*How you can respond:* "I know my worry might seem like it isn't a big deal, but it feels very real to me. Can you help me make a plan to feel calmer?"

Your goal now is to get your prefrontal cortex back in control. If you focus on calming your brain (breathing deeply, for example), you may be able to calm it enough to begin to make a plan (page 66) or to solve a problem.

## "You'll feel better if you just do it," or "You're probably just excited."

*When grown-ups say it:* When you get to school, when you're in line for a roller coaster, when you're running late for anything, when you're nervous about trying something new, when you don't want to do something most other kids are doing.

*Why it doesn't work:* You don't think adults can be absolutely sure you will be okay.

*Translation:* "I feel confident that if you just try the activity, you'll enjoy it."

*How you can respond:* "I might just be excited, but I still feel uncomfortable. Can we practice breathing together for a few minutes?"

Sometimes when grown-ups say this, it's actually true. If you are afraid to do something, but you do it anyway, you may see that it wasn't as frightening as you expected. And the symptoms of excitement can feel a lot like anxiety (see page 62). Still, there are many times we feel excitement *and* anxiety. One way to test whether you'll "feel better if you just do it" is to notice your surroundings. Are other people doing the thing you are afraid of? Do they look like they're feeling safe and happy? If so, it's most likely safe for you too. This is also a good time to use the strategies you read about in chapter 4 or any other strategies you've learned.

## "Aren't you a little old to be scared of that?" or "Nobody else looks worried."

*When grown-ups say it:* When they want you to join a group activity or do something they think you will enjoy.

*Why it doesn't work:* Everyone feels anxiety about different things, and anxiety doesn't care how old you are. Also, just because other kids don't *look* anxious doesn't mean they aren't. Most symptoms of anxiety can't be seen by others!

*Translation:* "I think you've grown a lot and you might be able to overcome this now." Also, "I might be feeling a little self-conscious that you and I are sticking out by not participating."

*How you can respond:* "Other people might be feeling worried too, but we just can't see it. I might feel better if I do a calming strategy. Will you help me, and then I can try joining the group?"

This is a good time to notice your surroundings (page 65) and make a plan for joining in.

## "See, that wasn't so hard," or "I told you it would be easy!"

*When grown-ups say it:* When you manage your anxiety so well that you are able to overcome it—you do the thing you were afraid of.

*Why it doesn't work:* Hello, managing anxiety is not easy! It takes lots of practice and lots of courage. When grown-ups say this, it can make it feel like all the work you did isn't recognized or appreciated.

*Translation:* "I know that was hard for you to do, and I'm so proud of you!"

*How you can respond:* "It takes a lot of work for me to overcome my anxiety. I'm proud of myself!"

Sometimes, just knowing what grown-ups really mean when they say these things can help. And sometimes, grown-ups say these things because they just don't understand or don't know what to say. You can self-advocate to let the adult know how you feel in these situations and what you need from them. You can also self-advocate to change how adults talk to you when you are experiencing anxiety. Pick a time to talk, then explain how you feel about the adult's words. You might ask them to instead use those moments of anxiety to show that they understand what you are feeling and to help you use your calming strategies.

# When to Listen to Your Gut (Even If You've Been Told Your Gut Overreacts)

Kids with anxiety get told all the time that they are overreacting or that they worry about everything. But sometimes your amygdala is right—there is danger. If your amygdala often sends false alarms, it can become difficult to know when you should listen to your symptoms. It's important to be able to tell the difference between anxiety and something really being dangerous.

## Is It Anxiety or a Real Danger?

Remember, your amygdala can't always tell the difference between a danger that is really happening and something you imagine could happen. Both cause the amygdala to send brain messages to get ready for danger. Sometimes your smart prefrontal cortex *knows* everything is okay, but it has trouble getting that message to your amygdala, so anxiety sticks around.

The good news is, when you are in real danger, your brain and body will often respond so quickly that you won't have time to think about it. When it counts, you can trust that your brain will keep you safe.

In situations where you don't need to react quite so quickly, you can use the strategies you learned in chapter 4 to calm your brain so that you can figure out whether what you are feeling is anxiety or a real danger.

Take a look at the following examples of times when you might feel anxiety and times when something dangerous is really happening.

**Anxiety:** There are matches in the house. You imagine someone could start a fire.

**Danger:** You see other kids lighting matches. They really are doing something that is dangerous.

**Anxiety:** If you go on a walk, you could see a dog who might bite.

**Danger:** A dog is growling at you. His aggressive behavior really could be a danger.

**Anxiety:** You imagine that if you go to a friend's party, someone could try to make you do something you don't want to do or don't feel comfortable doing.

**Danger:** A friend is actually asking you do something you know your parents would not want you to do.

**Anxiety:** If you go on a hike, you might come across poison oak and accidentally touch it.

**Danger:** You really did touch poison oak, which can give you a rash. It's time to change clothes and wash up quickly.

## How to Decide and What You Can Do

If possible, talk with an adult about your feelings. But if the possible danger is already happening, try to zoom out and name the things around you (page 65). This will help you and your smart prefrontal cortex get back in control and decide if what is happening is a true danger or if it's anxiety imagining what could happen.

**Important!** If you have decided something unsafe is happening, you should try to get away from the situation or end the danger. This might mean asking for an adult's help. One great idea is to talk with your parents (at a time when you are not worried) about how you should handle situations where there really is danger and how they can know that you truly need help. Some families pick a code word or a code phrase that kids can say to adults, over text or in a phone call, to signal that they need help getting out of a situation. If kids use that code word or phrase, the adults know that the kid has used their anxiety-taming strategies and has determined that something unsafe is happening. The adults need to help right away.

It can be difficult to know if something that makes you feel worried is anxiety or a real danger. But as you get better at managing anxiety (with strategies, therapy, or medication) and asking for what you need, you'll be able to think more clearly when you feel anxiety and feel confident in making good decisions.

When you self-advocate, you help others know what you need. You'll feel less alone in dealing with anxiety, and you'll get help a lot faster. Other people will appreciate that you explain your feelings and ask for what you need. They'll be happy to know what they can do to help.

# 8

# Before You Go

You've learned so much about anxiety! Hopefully, you've found some new strategies for managing anxiety, ways to talk about it, and techniques for advocating for yourself. You've also learned more about what happens if you go to therapy or take anxiety medication. There are just a couple more things to know before you go.

## Conditions That Often Coexist with Anxiety

Lots of kids have only anxiety. But it's also possible to have anxiety and something else. Here are some conditions that often coexist with anxiety:

- ADHD—A condition that makes it difficult to choose the focus of your attention and stay on task. About 25 percent of kids who have an anxiety disorder also have ADHD.

- Learning disorders (LD)—There are many learning disorders (or learning disabilities), but each is a condition that makes it difficult to learn and use certain skills, such as reading, writing, or math. About 28 percent of people with a learning disorder also have an anxiety disorder.

- Autism spectrum disorders (ASD)—People on the autism spectrum do not all have the same strengths or challenges, but many have difficulty with social skills, repetitive behaviors, and nonverbal communication (like interpreting facial expressions). About 40 percent of people with ASD also have an anxiety disorder.

- Another anxiety disorder—You may have social anxiety and panic disorder, for example. About 50 percent of people with one anxiety disorder have a second one. You can read about common anxiety disorders on page 34.

- Depression—Depression is a mood disorder that can make you feel sad or as though you don't have many feelings of any kind. People experiencing depression often find they don't enjoy things they used to. Up to 60 percent of people with an anxiety disorder also experience depression at some point.

Having anxiety and another condition may mean your treatment needs to be designed more specially for you. In some cases, treating the other condition makes a lot of anxiety go away.

# What It Feels Like to Be Less Worried

Working on strategies to manage your anxiety, going to therapy and/or taking medication, and learning to advocate for yourself really can make your life more awesome. When you've been very worried for a long time, it can be difficult to imagine life any other way. But when you are able to be in control and tell your amygdala to back off, and when you're able to ask for accommodations to help you do the things you need and want to do, amazing things can happen.

"I can focus on what my teachers say and actually get my work done."

"I can go anywhere without being worried that I'll have to take an escalator."

"I can go to my friend's house."

"I can open doors because I'm less worried about germs.*"

"I sleep in my own room every night."

"I eat more food now! My stomach doesn't hurt all the time."

"I can just hang out and have fun. I laugh more now."

*Sometimes extra care is needed to help us avoid getting sick. Talk to an adult to find ways to stay healthy without focusing on germs too much.

## Describing Yourself

Okay, so you have anxiety. And maybe up until now that has been a big focus of your life. You might even hear other people describe you as "a worrier," "sensitive," or "shy." But guess what? Anxiety is just one part of your life. There are other words that describe you too:

Smart  Hard worker

part of a family  Kind

Creative  ATHLETIC

ENERGETIC  Logical

Dramatic  Artistic

IMAGINATIVE  Funny

Caring  HELPFUL  MUSICAL

Good friend  Thoughtful

What other words describe you?

# The End

You read the whole book! Either that, or you skipped to this page to find out how it would end. So here's how it ends: You have lots of new tools now for understanding anxiety, managing it, and talking to people to get what you need. You've also learned a lot (more than many people know) about how therapy works and what medication can do to help with anxiety.

You might want to put this book someplace where it will be easy for you to find it again. In a few days or weeks, you might want to check back to remember exactly how to do a certain strategy, or to remind yourself what's happening in your brain when you feel anxiety. You can put bookmarks in here or sticky notes on pages that you want to revisit quickly. Heck, take a highlighter to it or color in some pictures. It's your book—you get to be in control. Just like with anxiety.

# A Note to Adults

I'm not a mental health professional, and this book is not designed to take the place of therapy or any expert opinion. What I am is a parent of a child with anxiety, and a writer and editor by profession. I've spent countless hours reading about anxiety, reading about parenting, and reading about parenting an anxious child. I've also introduced (and reintroduced) my daughter to all the elements of this book over her life, and we've sat together in the name of anxiety in the offices of one pediatrician, one therapist, four psychologists, and two psychiatrists. Each was helpful. And each made me realize my child needed (and deserved) more information to get on board with our plan to help her with anxiety.

I've written this book to help kids understand what is happening in their brains and why adults are asking them to work on managing anxiety—by practicing strategies, going to therapy, and/or taking medication. Some kids are eager to become less anxious. Other kids feel their anxiety is essential; they believe it keeps them safe, or they've felt it for so long that it has become part of their identity. And still others might not want to talk about anxiety at all because it makes them feel even more anxiety. For some kids, the explanations of anxiety and its treatment that adults usually give aren't enough. They need to understand more. This book is for them!

I've included a simplified explanation of how anxiety works in the brain, the real names of brain sections and neurotransmitters, definitions of common childhood anxiety disorders, descriptions of what takes place in a therapist's office, and information on how the most commonly prescribed anxiety medications work—things you might not typically see in a book for kids. If information is power, then this book should empower your child to work with you and professionals to take control back from anxiety.

A few points:

- Psychologist Myles L. Cooley, Ph.D., has reviewed some of the information in this book. He has evaluated and treated children, adolescents, and adults for more than 30 years. Dr. Cooley serves as a consultant to schools and has presented educational programs to educators, mental health professionals, physicians, and parents.

- Through most of this book, I use *anxiety* as noun rather than the adjective *anxious*. This is a small part of my effort to make anxiety a "thing" your child deals with rather than a part of them they can't control.

- You might want to read this book too. You may not know what to expect in a therapist's office or how medications for anxiety work. And if you haven't had much experience with anxiety yourself, you may not fully understand what's happening in your child's brain. If you do read it before your child, though, do me a favor and play it cool. I find books like this are more likely to be read by tweens if we "accidentally" leave them in a well-trafficked part of the house.

# Glossary

**Accommodation:** An adjustment or adaptation to fit a person's needs. An accommodation is an adjustment to how you'll do something at school, home, etc., while you work on managing anxiety.

**Advocate:** To support or champion another person's cause or needs. A person who does this is also called an advocate.

**Amygdala:** An almond-shaped section of the brain that plays a role in emotional responses, including anxiety.

**Anxiety:** A feeling of worry about something uncertain, something that could happen, or something that you imagine happening.

**Assertive:** Having confident statements and behavior.

**Brainstorm:** Thinking of ideas or solutions.

**Cognitive behavioral therapy (CBT):** A form of therapy in which you learn ways to change your thinking so you can take control of anxiety. CBT is considered the most effective type of therapy for anxiety.

**Diagnosis:** An official name for the cause of your symptoms, given by an expert.

**Disorder:** A word to mean that something is not working normally or the way we would hope.

**Excessive:** In excess, or more than needed.

**Exposure:** To expose or be in contact with something.

**Exposure and response prevention therapy (ERP):** A form of cognitive behavioral therapy that is often used for obsessive-compulsive disorder. ERP works by gradually exposing yourself to a thing (or situation) that makes you feel anxiety and learning to tolerate that feeling until it decreases or goes away.

**Fight, flight, or freeze:** The brain's natural or instinctive responses to a threat.

**Heredity:** The passing of physical or mental traits from one generation to the next.

**Hypothalamus:** Your brain's control center for hunger, temperature, emotional activity, and other functions.

**Intense/Intensity:** Words commonly used when talking about symptoms. An intense symptom is a strong symptom.

**Irrational:** Unreasonable, or not using "good sense."

**Neurotransmitter:** Chemical substances that transmit messages in your brain.

**Phobia:** An extreme or irrational fear of a particular thing.

**Prefrontal cortex:** A section in the front of the brain responsible for processing information from the other regions and making decisions about behavior, solving problems, and focusing attention.

**Proportional:** A reaction size that "matches" the size of what is happening. A disproportional amount of worry would be a lot of worry about something that is not very dangerous.

**Ruminate:** To repeat over and over.

**Self-advocacy:** Explaining the reason something is difficult and asking for help to make it possible for you to do it. A person who practices self-advocacy is called a self-advocate.

**Serotonin:** A chemical made in your brain. Serotonin is name of the brain message your prefrontal cortex sends to the amygdala to tell it that everything is okay and it can stop freaking out now. Serotonin is made in your brain and digestive tract.

**SSRI:** Selective Serotonin Reuptake Inhibitor. The most commonly prescribed medications for anxiety and depression.

**Strategy:** A way to help your brain know that everything is okay and it can calm down now.

**Symptom:** A sign or signal about what's going on in a person's brain or body.

**Therapist:** Also called a counselor. A person who helps others with mental health issues. Therapists are trained to know about the brain and human behavior. Could be a licensed therapist, a psychologist, or psychiatrist.

**Therapy:** A regular appointment—like a class—where you get to work on ways to train your brain to manage anxiety.

**Transition:** Whenever one thing is ending and another is beginning.

**Treatment:** Working with a mental health professional on learning to manage anxiety or another challenge.

# Resources

## For Kids

### Books

*All Birds Have Anxiety* by Kathy Hoopmann (Philadelphia: Jessica Kingsley Publishers, 2017). A fun book comparing bird behavior to human anxiety.

*The Anxiety Workbook for Teens: Activities to Help You Deal with Anxiety and Worry* by Lisa M. Schab, L.C.S.W. (Oakland, CA: Instant Help Books, 2008). Activities to help older kids manage anxiety and better understand their symptoms.

*Guts* by Raina Telgemeier (New York: Graphix, 2019). Fictional graphic novel based on the author's real childhood fear of throwing up and how she dealt with her fear.

*Outsmarting Worry: An Older Kid's Guide to Managing Anxiety* by Dawn Huebner, Ph.D. (Philadelphia: Jessica Kingsley Publishers, 2018). Teaches skills to face and overcome anxiety.

*A Smart Girl's Guide to Worry: How to Feel Less Stressed and Have More Fun* by Judy Woodburn and Nancy Holyoke (Middleton, WI: American Girl Publishing, 2016). Facts and tips about worry, specifically for girls.

*Something Bad Happened: A Kid's Guide to Coping with Events in the News* by Dawn Huebner, Ph.D. (London: Jessica Kingsley Publishers, 2020). Guides kids and the adults in their lives through tough conversations about serious world events.

*Standing Up to OCD Workbook for Kids* by Tyson Reuter, Ph.D. (Emeryville, CA: Rockridge Press, 2019). Book featuring 40 activities to help kids manage OCD.

*The Survival Guide for Making and Being Friends* by James J. Crist, Ph.D. (Minneapolis: Free Spirit Publishing, 2014). Tools, quizzes, and advice from kids about making friends to help boost confidence in kids with social anxiety.

*What to Do When You Don't Want to Be Apart: A Kid's Guide to Overcoming Separation Anxiety* by Kristen Lavallee, Ph.D., and Silvia Schneider, Dr. rer. nat. (Washington, DC: Magination Press, 2017). Teaches skills for younger kids dealing with separation anxiety.

*What to Do When You Dread Your Bed: A Kid's Guide to Overcoming Problems with Sleep* by Dawn Huebner, Ph.D. (Washington, DC: Magination Press, 2008). Teaches skills for younger kids dealing with fear of sleeping on their own.

*What to Do When You Worry Too Much: A Kid's Guide to Overcoming Anxiety* by Dawn Huebner, Ph.D. (Washington, DC: Magination Press, 2005). Teaches kids and parents cognitive-behavioral skills used in the treatment of anxiety.

*What to Do When You're Scared and Worried: A Guide for Kids* by James J. Crist, Ph.D. (Minneapolis: Free Spirit Publishing, 2004). Advice, reassurance, and ideas for kids with hard-to-handle fears.

### Apps

Headspace (headspace.com). Mindfulness and meditation app. Most meditations require a paid subscription but some are available for free.

### Videos

"Fight Flight Freeze—A Guide to Anxiety for Kids" by Anxiety Canada
youtu.be/FfSbWc3O_5M

"5 Tips for Coping with Test Anxiety (for Kids!)" by Mylemarks.
youtu.be/sDYx9qM_ygg

## For Parents

### Books

*Anxious Kids, Anxious Parents: 7 Ways to Stop the Worry Cycle and Raise Courageous and Independent Children* by Reid Wilson, Ph.D., and Lynn Lyons, L.I.C.S.W. (Deerfield Beach, FL: Health Communications Inc., 2013). Guides parents through skills to help their child work through anxieties.

*Anxiety Relief for Kids: On-the-Spot Strategies to Help Your Child Overcome Worry, Panic, and Avoidance* by Bridget Flynn Walker, Ph.D. (Oakland, CA: New Harbinger Publications, 2017). Learn more about anxiety, how to identify the ways your child is coping with anxiety, and interventions to help your child.

*Little Panic: Dispatches from an Anxious Life* by Amanda Stern (New York: Grand Central Publishing, 2018). Memoir of the author's childhood with panic disorder and an excellent window into the mind of a child with anxiety.

*Panic Free: The 10-Day Program to End Panic, Anxiety, and Claustrophobia* by Tom Bunn (Novato, CA: New World Library, 2019). A short-term program to learn to manage a specific phobia or panic trigger. Written for adults, but parents can work through it with their child.

### Podcasts

*Your Anxious Child: 5-Minute Solutions with Edward Plimpton, Ph.D.* Quick episodes target various aspects of anxiety and offer techniques parents can utilize with their kids.

*Dear Anxiety.* Research-based solutions for mental wellness.

### Websites

Brightly (readbrightly.com). Reading suggestions and lists, including 12 kid-approved middle grade books that tackle mental health.

Child Mind Institute (childmind.org). Accurate information on a wealth of topics to empower families to get help.

Hey Sigmund (heysigmund.com). The latest in psychology made understandable for laypeople. Articles often deal with current events that may impact mental health.

Understood (understood.org). Explanations of learning and thinking differences and helpful articles that explain diagnoses, treatments, and everyday challenges such as managing school.

# Bibliography

## General

Bunn, Tom. *Panic Free: The 10-Day Program to End Panic, Anxiety, and Claustrophobia*. New World Library, 2019.

CDC. "Children's Mental Health." Centers for Disease Control and Prevention, updated June 15, 2020, cdc.gov /childrensmentalhealth/data.html.

Gadye, Levi. "What Part of the Brain Deals with Anxiety? What Can Brains Affected by Anxiety Tell Us?" BrainFacts.org, June 29, 2018, brainfacts.org/diseases-and-disorders/mental-health/2018 /what-part-of-the-brain-deals-with-anxiety-what-can-brains -affected-by-anxiety-tell-us-062918.

Greenberg, Melanie. "Understanding Brain Circuits of Fear, Stress, and Anxiety." Psychology Today, September 30, 2019, psychologytoday.com/us/blog/the-mindful-self-express/201909 /understanding-brain-circuits-fear-stress-and-anxiety.

Harvard Health. "Understanding the Stress Response." Harvard Medical School, updated July 6, 2020, health.harvard.edu /staying-healthy/understanding-the-stress-response.

Huebner, Dawn. *Outsmarting Worry: An Older Kid's Guide to Managing Anxiety*. Jessica Kingsley Publishers, 2017.

Walker, Bridget Flynn. *Anxiety Relief for Kids: On-the-Spot Strategies to Help Your Child Overcome Worry, Panic and Avoidance*. New Harbinger Publications, 2017.

## Anxiety and the Brain

Bezdek, Kylie Garber, and Eva H. Telzer. "Have No Fear, the Brain Is Here! How Your Brain Responds to Stress." Frontiers for Young Minds, December 20, 2017, kids.frontiersin.org/article/10.3389 /frym.2017.00071.

Pittman, Catherine M., and Jamie L. Rathert. "Explaining Anxiety in the Brain: Explanations for Children and Adults that Enhance Treatment Compliance in a Whole Brain Approach." Anxiety Disorders Association of American 32nd Annual Conference, April 14, 2012, adaa.org/sites/default/files/Pittman%20158.pdf.

## Mindfulness Basics
Kind, Shelley, and Stefan G. Hofmann. "Facts About the Effects of Mindfulness." Anxiety.org, accessed August 19, 2020, anxiety.org /can-mindfulness-help-reduce-anxiety.

## How Therapy Works
Gelb, Suzanne. "What Really Happens in a Therapy Session." Psychology Today, December 5, 2015, psychologytoday.com/us /blog/all-grown/201512/what-really-happens-in-therapy-session.

## Science and Medicine
The Brain from Top to Bottom. "The Amygdala and Its Allies." Accessed August 19, 2020, thebrain.mcgill.ca/flash/d/d_04/d_04 _cr/d_04_cr_peu/d_04_cr_peu.html.

Camilleri, Michael. "Serotonin in the Gastrointestinal Tract." *Current Opinion in Endocrinology, Diabetes, and Obesity*, February 2009, 16(1): 53–59, ncbi.nlm.nih.gov/pmc/articles/PMC2694720.

CDC. "Anxiety and Depression." Centers for Disease Control and Prevention, updated March 30, 2020, cdc.gov /childrensmentalhealth/depression.html.

Comninos, Andreas. "Your Brain's Threat System." Mindfulness & Clinical Psychology Solutions, accessed August 19, 2020, mi-psych.com.au/your-brains-threat-system.

Khan Academy. "Neurotransmitters and Receptors." Accessed August 19, 2020, khanacademy.org/science/biology /human-biology/neuron-nervous-system/a/neurotransmitters -their-receptors.

McIntosh, James, and Debra Rose Wilson. "What Is Serotonin and What Does It Do?" Medical News Today, February 2, 2018, medicalnewstoday.com/articles/232248.

Young, Simon N. "How to Increase Serotonin in the Human Brain without Drugs." *Journal of Psychiatry and Neuroscience*, November 2007, 32(6): 394–399, ncbi.nlm.nih.gov/pmc/articles/PMC2077351.

### Types of Anxiety

ADAA. "Childhood Anxiety Disorders." Anxiety and Depression Association of America, updated September 2015, adaa.org/living-with-anxiety/children/childhood-anxiety-disorders.

Child Mind Institute. "Panic Disorder Basics." Accessed August 19, 2020, childmind.org/guide/panic-disorder.

### Sleep

AAP. "AAP Supports Childhood Sleep Guidelines." American Academy of Pediatrics, June 13, 2016, healthychildren.org/English/news/Pages/AAP-Supports-Childhood-Sleep-Guidelines.aspx.

Goldstein, Andrea N., Stephanie M. Greer, Jared M. Saletin, Allison G. Harvey, Jack B. Nitschke, and Matthew P. Walker. "Tired and Apprehensive: Anxiety Amplifies the Impact of Sleep Loss on Aversive Brain Anticipation." *The Journal of Neuroscience*, June 26, 2013, 33(26): 10607–10615, jneurosci.org/content/33/26/10607.

Saghir, Zahid, Javeria N. Syeda, Adnan S. Muhammad, and Tareg H. Balla Abdalla. "The Amygdala, Sleep Debt, Sleep Deprivation, and the Emotion of Anger: A Possible Connection?" *Cureus*, July 2018, 10(7): e2912, ncbi.nlm.nih.gov/pmc/articles/PMC6122651.

Tamminen, Jakke. "How a Lack of Sleep Affects Your Brain—and Personality." The Conversation, October 17, 2016, theconversation.com/how-a-lack-of-sleep-affects-your-brain-and-personality-66604.

Webster, Molly. "Can You Catch Up on Lost Sleep?" *Scientific American*, May 6, 2008, scientificamerican.com / article / fact-or-fiction-can-you-catch-up-on-sleep.

## Conditions That Coexist with Anxiety

Cameron, Oliver G. "Understanding Comorbid Depression and Anxiety." Psychiatric Times, December 1, 2007, psychiatrictimes.com / articles / understanding-comorbid -depression-and-anxiety.

D'Agati, Elisa, Paolo Curatolo, and Luigi Mazzone. "Comorbidity Between ADHD and Anxiety Disorders Across the Lifespan." *International Journal of Psychiatry in Clinical Practice*, June 24, 2019, 23(4): 238–244, ncbi.nlm.nih.gov / pubmed / 31232613.

Hirschfeld, Robert M. A. "The Comorbidity of Major Depression and Anxiety Disorders: Recognition and Management in Primary Care." *The Primary Care Companion to the Journal Of Clinical Psychiatry*, 2001, 3(6): 244–254, ncbi.nlm.nih.gov / pmc / articles / PMC181193.

Margari, Lucia, Maura Buttiglione, Francesco Craig, Arcangelo Cristella, Concetta de Giambattista, Emilia Matera, Francesca Operto, and Marta Simone. "Neuropathological Comorbidities in Learning Disorders." *BMC Neurology*, December 2013, 13: 198, ncbi.nlm.nih.gov / pmc / articles / PMC3878726.

Noyes, Russell Jr. "Comorbidity in Generalized Anxiety Disorder." *Psychiatric Clinics of North America*, March 2001, 24(1): 41–55, ncbi.nlm.nih.gov / pubmed / 11225508.

Zaboski, Brian A., and Eric A. Storch. "Comorbid Autism Spectrum Disorder and Anxiety Disorders: A Brief Review." *Future Neurology*, February 2018, 13(1): 31–37, ncbi.nlm.nih.gov / pubmed / 29379397.

# Index

# About the Author

**Summer Batte** is a magazine editor, writer, and parent who has spent more than a decade learning about anxiety. She earned her bachelor's degree in psychology from Stanford University and lives in the San Francisco Bay Area with her husband and daughter.

# Other Great Resources from Free Spirit

### What to Do When You're Scared & Worried
A Guide for Kids
*by James J. Crist, Ph.D.*

For ages 9–13.
*128 pp.; PB; 2-color; illust.;
5⅜" x 8⅜".*

### What to Do When You're Cranky & Blue
A Guide for Kids
*by James J. Crist, Ph.D.*

For ages 9–13.
*128 pp.; PB; 2-color; illust.;
5⅜" x 8⅜".*

### The Survival Guide for Making and Being Friends
*by James J. Crist, Ph.D.*

For ages 8–13.
*128 pp.; PB; 2-color; illust.;
6" x 9".*

### The Survival Guide for Kids with ADHD
(Updated Edition)
*by John F. Taylor, Ph.D.*

For ages 8–12.
*128 pp.; PB; 2-color; illust.;
6" x 9".*

### Fighting Invisible Tigers
Stress Management for Teens (Revised & Updated 4th Edition)
*by Earl Hipp*

For ages 11 & up.
*144 pp.; PB; 2-color; illust.;
6" x 9".*

### When a Friend Dies
A Book for Teens About Grieving & Healing
(Updated 3rd Edition)
*by Marilyn E. Gootman, Ed.D.*

For ages 11 & up.
*136 pp.; PB; B&W photos;
5" x 7".*

---

**Interested in purchasing multiple quantities and receiving volume discounts?**
Contact edsales@freespirit.com or call 1.800.735.7323 and ask for Education Sales.

**Many Free Spirit authors are available for speaking engagements, workshops, and keynotes.**
Contact speakers@freespirit.com or call 1.800.735.7323.

For pricing information, to place an order, or to request a free catalog, contact:

**Free Spirit Publishing • 6325 Sandburg Road, Suite 100 • Minneapolis, MN 55427-3674
toll-free 800.735.7323 • local 612.338.2068 • fax 612.337.5050
help4kids@freespirit.com • freespirit.com**